CH

D0349640

Lifeline
BIOGRAPHIES

JOHNNY DEPP
Hollywood Rebel

by Matt Doeden

Twenty-First Century Books · Minneapolis

Twenty-First Century Books
A division of Lerner Publishing Group, Inc.
241 First Avenue North
Minneapolis, MN 55401 U.S.A.

Website address: www.lernerbooks.com

Library of Congress Cataloging-in-Publication Data

Doeden, Matt.
    Johnny Depp : Hollywood rebel / by Matt Doeden.
        p.   cm. — (USA TODAY lifeline biographies)
    Includes bibliographical references and index.
    Includes filmography.
    ISBN 978–0–7613–6420–7 (lib. bdg. : alk. paper)
    1. Depp, Johnny—Juvenile literature. 2. Motion picture actors and actresses—United States—Biography—Juvenile literature. I. Title.
    PN2287.D39D64 2011
    791.4302'8092—dc22 [B]   2010017624

Manufactured in the United States of America
1 – VI – 12/31/10

USA TODAY
Lifeline
BIOGRAPHIES

USA TODAY

INTRODUCTION

Here's Johnny: Johnny Depp was a struggling actor and former punk rock musician in the mid-1980s.

Reluctant Star

In 1986 not many people knew the name Johnny Depp. The twenty-three-year-old was a former punk rocker and a struggling actor. He'd appeared in several movies but had yet to distinguish himself. Johnny had thought that he'd gotten his big break by landing a part in the 1986 Oscar-winning movie *Platoon*. But his role in the film was so brief that hardly anyone noticed him.

But television executive Patrick Hasburgh had noticed. Hasburgh was developing a TV series about police officers going undercover in high schools. The show was initially called *Jump Street Chapel*. It was later renamed *21 Jump Street*. Hasburgh wanted Johnny to play the role of Tom Hanson, one of the police officers.

Johnny saw himself as a big-screen actor, not a television actor. So he turned down the role. The series began filming a pilot (first episode) with actor Jeff Yagher playing Hanson. But Yagher didn't work out in the role. Hasburgh had a problem. The Fox television network was asking for more episodes of *21 Jump Street*, but he had nobody to play Hanson.

Once again, Hasburgh asked Johnny. And again, Johnny bristled at the idea. He needed the work, but he didn't want to sign a long contract that would tie him up for years. Finally, Johnny's agent convinced him to do it. "My agent said the average span of a TV series is 13 episodes, if that. One season. So I said OK."

21 Jump Street: Depp *(left)* co-starred in the hit TV show *21 Jump Street* with Peter DeLuise *(center)* and Dustin Nguyen *(right)*.

It was a decision that would change Johnny's life. He signed a six-year contract that paid him $45,000 per episode. Johnny had never had that kind of money before. And he didn't really expect the role, or the show, to last nearly that long.

He was wrong. The show was a hit, and Johnny was the main attraction. He was an overnight sensation. Suddenly, reporters wanted to talk to him. Teenaged girls screamed at the sight of him. He was on the covers of magazines. The show grew and grew in popularity. It was renewed for a second season, then for a third. Johnny's popularity showed no signs of dropping off. He was a teen idol.

Johnny had money and fame. For many actors, this would have been a dream come true. But not for Johnny. He didn't want to be a TV star. He didn't want to be a teen idol. He didn't like his own show, and he hated the character he played. He found the idea of the police running undercover operations in

Unhappy: Depp had great success in the late 1980s with his role on *21 Jump Street*, but he wasn't happy with it. He wanted to act in movies instead.

high schools to be offensive. But the contract he'd so reluctantly signed left him few options. Like it or not, he had to be Tom Hanson, even if it made him miserable.

"Once you put your name on a [contract], you have no choice," Johnny later said of his situation. "There are people in ties with very big pens and hulking desks who do bad things to you [if you don't honor your obligations]".

And so Johnny waited. He knew that in time, *21 Jump Street* would run its course. And then he could use his newfound fame to become the actor that he really wanted to be.

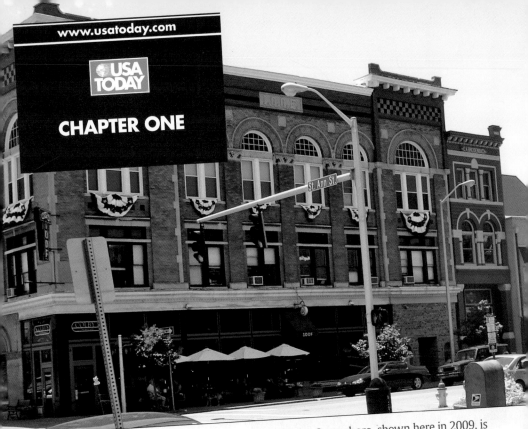

Hometown: Depp was born in Owensboro, Kentucky. Owensboro, shown here in 2009, is in northwestern Kentucky.

Young Rebel

John Christopher Depp was born June 9, 1963, in Owensboro, Kentucky. He was the fourth child of Betty Sue Depp, and her second child with husband John Depp. John Jr., or Johnny, had a sister, Elisa (two), nicknamed Christie; and two half-siblings, Deborah (seven) and Daniel (nine).

Johnny's family was middle class—not rich, but not poor either. His father worked as a civil engineer, while Betty Sue was a waitress. Johnny's earliest memories were of the late 1960s and early 1970s. These were turbulent times in the United States and across the world. The civil rights movement—the demand for equal treatment for African Americans and other minorities—was in full force. U.S. combat involvement in the Vietnam War, which had dragged on from 1964 into the 1970s, was becoming increasingly less popular.

Johnny's childhood was, in some ways, equally unstable. For some reason, the Depp family never stayed put for long. Johnny's early

Mother and son: Depp *(left)* and his mother, Betty Sue Depp *(right)*, are shown here in 1990.

life included a long string of household moves. Friends were hard to make and harder to keep.

"We moved constantly," Johnny later said. "My mom just liked to move for some reason. It was hard. Depending on how far we'd move, you'd have to make new friends. We never stayed in one neighborhood for long."

When Johnny was seven years old, the family moved to Miramar, Florida. Once there, the moving got even worse. The family moved from apartment to apartment, motel to motel. Johnny felt more and more isolated. For a time, he stopped even trying to make friends. "I always felt like a total freak," he said.

Like any kid, Johnny was filled with wild ideas. For a time, he was determined to become the first white member of the Harlem

Globetrotters basketball team. He dreamed of being like motorcycle daredevil Evel Knieval. Or maybe he'd become a spy, a rock star, a SWAT team member, or any number of fantastic jobs. Wild behavior went right along with his ideas. He was once suspended from school for pulling down his pants and showing his rear end to a teacher. Another time he burned his face trying to breathe fire by blowing gasoline onto a burning broomstick—a stunt that earned him a scar on his right cheek. He blamed his fierce independence on his Native American heritage—one of his grandfathers was a full-blooded Cherokee.

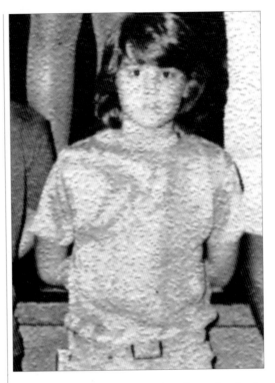

Young Johnny: Depp, shown here in grade school, got into trouble in school for wild behavior.

Troubled Teen

Johnny's independent, and often troublemaking, spirit only grew as he matured into a teenager. His home life certainly wasn't helping matters. Over the years, his parents had grown apart and spent much of their time arguing. They weren't happy, and neither was Johnny. It showed in Johnny's behavior. He started hanging out with other troubled kids. Theft and vandalism were among his petty crimes as an early teen.

Johnny entered high school but had little interest in his classes. He was much more interested in music. He spent much of his time learning to play the electric guitar. "I became obsessed with the guitar," he later said. "I locked myself in my bedroom for the better part of a year and taught myself chords. I'd try to learn things off records."

Soon, Johnny joined some other kids in a garage band called Flame. Johnny and the band experimented with drugs, sex, and alcohol.

"I felt completely and utterly confused by everything that was going on around me," Johnny later said of his teenage years. "I didn't get any of it. It wasn't so much that I felt outside of something as much as I didn't feel inside of something and didn't want to, either. I saw these boys and girls competing for most popular this and that, the Prom Queen or the Prom King, and it was like, 'What [nonsense].'"

When Johnny was fifteen, his parents finally divorced. Johnny chose to live with his mother, who was taking the divorce badly. It was a tough time. Betty Sue suffered a nervous breakdown. Johnny realized that she needed him, and it was time to grow up. He was ready to put all of his energy into a music career.

Punk Rock Dreams

Johnny had flunked out of Miramar High School, but he didn't view that as a problem. He was focused on becoming a punk rock star. In 1980 Johnny formed a band called the Kids. The Kids used alcohol and illegal drugs, but it wasn't the same kind of destructive influence on Johnny that Flame had been. As Johnny's family life continued to fall apart, the band became something of a home away from home.

The Kids was a minor success, booking gigs at local clubs, parties, and anywhere else they could. Over the next three years, the band's reputation grew. Soon they were opening for bigger acts such as Iggy Pop, the B-52s and the Talking Heads. In 1983 a booking agent invited them to come to Los Angeles, California, and play at a club called the Palace. It was an opportunity they couldn't resist. Johnny and his bandmates packed their bags.

Johnny got into his share of trouble in his teenage years. He later explained why he acted out. "I did my share of despicable stuff," he said. "I don't see what I was doing as a kid as 'bad boy.' What I was doing was out of boredom. I dropped out of school because I was bored with it. All I had on my mind was playing the guitar. . . . I wasn't a mean kid who did a lot of crime. It's not like I would run down the street and grab an old lady's purse. Anything I did was never malicious."

But Johnny had some personal business to attend to first. He had met a girl, Lori Anne Allison, and the two were getting married. Allison was the sister of one of Johnny's bandmates. She was also a musician, although she worked as a makeup artist. She was five years older than Johnny, but that mattered little to the couple. They married in Florida and then prepared to head to California.

Marrying young: Depp and Lori Anne Allison *(shown here in 1997)* married in Florida in 1983 before moving to California.

And so, twenty-year-old Johnny, complete with earrings, a head of wild hair, tattoos, and a new bride, headed for the West Coast. He had dreams of making it big there, of becoming a true music star. But the music scene in Los Angeles proved difficult to crack. The competition for gigs was fierce. The Kids were exciting up-and-comers in Florida. But in southern California, they were just another unknown band. According to some, the Kids' sound lacked originality. Nothing set them apart from the crowd. They struggled even to make enough money for food.

Johnny took a wide range of jobs to pay the bills. He spent time as a construction worker, gas station attendant, telephone salesperson, and more. Life in California wasn't all that Johnny had dreamed it would be. The Kids changed their name to Six Gun Method but still struggled to gain any sort of recognition. Most of Johnny's free time went to the band, leaving Lori alone more often than not. The marriage became strained. Less than two years after the wedding, the couple split. "I was a child of divorce," Johnny later admitted. "I didn't know how a marriage worked."

Nightmare

Johnny and Lori remained friends. She introduced him to her new boyfriend, actor Nicolas Coppola. Coppola went by the stage name Nicolas Cage. Cage was the nephew of famous director Francis Ford Coppola. Johnny and Cage became friends, and Cage encouraged Johnny to give acting a try. Cage went so far as to set up an interview for Johnny with agent Ilene Feldman.

Twenty-one-year-old Johnny grudgingly went to the interview. He did not make much of a first impression. Feldman later said that Johnny just didn't seem interested. But his youthful good looks caught Feldman's eye. Behind the long hair and earrings, she saw a face that she could market. She sent Johnny to an audition for a film being planned by director Wes Craven. *A Nightmare on Elm Street* was a slash-'em-up horror movie. Craven was looking for fresh young faces

Acting friends: Depp *(right)* met actor Nicolas Cage *(left)* through Depp's ex-wife. The two became friends, and Cage convinced Depp to try acting.

to die at the hands of the movie's monster, Freddy Krueger. In the story, Krueger is a child murderer who is killed by a mob of angry parents. Years later, he returns from the grave to get revenge by tormenting the mob's children, now teenagers, in their dreams.

Johnny was auditioning for the role of Glen Lantz, the boyfriend of the main character. There was a problem, however. The script called for an all-American boy—tall, blond, and strong. That description didn't fit Johnny at all.

"[Glen] was described as this big blonde surfer jock type," Johnny recalled, "and here I was, this scrawny, pale little guy, with long hair starched to death with five-day old hairspray."

Still, Johnny's dark, brooding manner and good looks made an impression. Craven's sixteen-year-old daughter was smitten, and she convinced her father to cast Johnny in the role.

Nightmare was no guaranteed success. After all, it was just another teenage slasher flick. It could have been the sort of movie that is forgotten almost as soon as it's released. But it didn't work out that way. Surprisingly, the movie garnered some critical praise. It also attracted something of a cult following and went on to spawn sequel after sequel.

USA TODAY Snapshots®

Some fava beans with that?
Whom Americans view as Hollywood's scariest villains:

Hannibal Lecter, *Silence of the Lambs*
22.9%

Freddy Krueger, *A Nightmare on Elm Street*
17%

Michael Myers, *Halloween*
16.1%

Source: Redbox survey of 630 video-rental customers Oct. 7-11

By Melanie Eversley and Adrienne Lewis, USA TODAY, 2007

But the sequels did Johnny little good, since Glen dies in the first movie. And according to most critics, Johnny's performance was less than stellar. Some critics complained that he mumbled through the part. He often delivered his lines too quickly and showed little emotion during his scenes. Reports said that Craven had to cut back Glen's dialogue from the original script. The director knew Johnny was out of his element, and he did his best to cover for the first-time actor.

"Doing *A Nightmare on Elm Street* was a trial-by-fire sort of thing," Johnny explained. "I'd never acted before. I'd never done school plays. Nothing. The fact that it was totally new to me was a tremendous challenge."

In short, Johnny looked very much like a musician trying to act. And after all the time he spent on the *Nightmare* set, he was now a musician without a band. Six Gun Method had been barely getting by before, and with Johnny's absence, the rest of the members decided enough was enough. They split up.

The Nightmare Saga

No one could have guessed it at the time, but Wes Craven's *A Nightmare on Elm Street* sparked a long franchise of celebrated slasher movies. The first film had a budget of less than $2 million. But it earned more than $25 million at the box office. A sequel was all but guaranteed. And the sequels kept coming.

With the release of *A Nightmare on Elm Street* (the 2010 version), a total of nine *Nightmare* movies had been made. This total includes 2003's *Freddy vs. Jason*, in which Krueger faces off with the murderous Jason character from the *Friday the 13th* movies. An independent film company called New Line Cinema released the original and the sequels. The *Nightmare* movies helped build New Line into a major film studio.

The Nightmare franchise extends far beyond just films, however.

Iconic role: Robert Englund played Freddy Krueger in most of the *Nighmare* movies.

It spawned a short-lived TV show called *Freddy's Nightmares*, comic books, a series of novels, and several video games. That little 1984 slasher film went on to launch one of the biggest film franchises of all time.

The Acting Bug

With his music career sidelined, Johnny decided that acting was his future. He attended acting classes in Los Angeles. He also appeared in a short student film titled *Dummies*. In the film, he played the boyfriend of actress Sherilyn Fenn. The two hit it off, and once again, Johnny was in love. Before long, the couple was engaged to be married.

It didn't take long for Johnny to land another movie role. He was cast in the comedy *Private Resort* (1985). The movie was an outrageous (and, by most accounts, pointless) farce about two young men (Johnny and Rob Morrow) who go to a hotel to chase women. The movie was forgettable in almost all respects, and Johnny hated it. He dismissed it simply as, "a stupid film."

Hollywood girlfriend: Depp met actress Sherilyn Fenn on the set of the student movie *Dummies* (1985). They eventually got engaged. She is shown here in 1988.

Things didn't get much better with *Slow Burn*, a made-for-TV mystery. Johnny played the kidnapped son of a millionaire. As in *Nightmare*, Johnny's biggest contribution to the film was the death of his character.

Johnny's acting career seemed to be going nowhere fast. All he was getting were forgettable roles in mostly forgettable films. That was about to change.

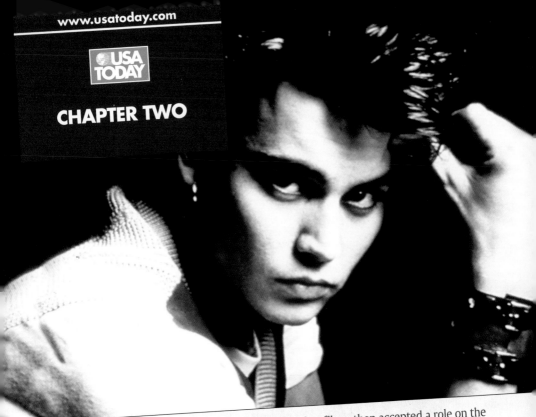

From film to television: Depp had small roles in a few films, then accepted a role on the Fox TV show *21 Jump Street* in 1987.

Rising Star

In 1985 Johnny auditioned for the war drama *Platoon*. The director, Oliver Stone, was a veteran of the Vietnam War. He wanted to make a film that truly showed what the experience had been like. Stone was a rising star in Hollywood, known for his hard-hitting approach and controversial style. *Platoon* was loaded with young talent, including the lead actor, Charlie Sheen. Johnny made a good impression in his audition and landed the role of Lerner, an interpreter.

Johnny was eager to take on the role. He visited with his uncle Bobby, who had served in Vietnam, to get a better sense of his character. Then he boarded a plane and headed off to the Philippines for filming. In the movie, the Philippine Islands' lush rain forests stood in for the jungles of Vietnam.

Stone was determined that his cast be prepared, so he put them through a strenuous boot camp. Johnny and his castmates had to learn what it was like to train for the military. The cast went through heavy physical training. They got very little sleep. By the time Stone started filming, all the actors were exhausted—exactly the way Stone wanted them to be. A well-rested and relaxed cast couldn't convincingly portray soldiers, Stone reasoned. He needed his men tired and stressed out, as real soldiers would be.

Filming *Platoon* was a difficult process. The cast worked twelve- and fourteen-hour days under harsh jungle conditions. But to Johnny,

Boot camp: Depp *(far right)* has said he learned a lot while filming Oliver Stone's movie *Platoon* in 1985. The actors in the film, including Tom Berenger *(center)*, had to go through military boot camp to train for their roles.

it was a learning experience. He got a chance to work alongside some of Hollywood's top actors. Even though his part in the movie was minor, he felt it would be the kind of exposure that would really help his career. This was a powerful, well-written script. It opened to record audiences in February 1987 and would go on to win the Academy Award for Best Motion Picture. It got rave reviews from critics and casual movie fans alike.

But the news wasn't all good for Johnny. Lerner had always been a small part in the movie. During editing, most of Johnny's lines were cut from the film. What started as a small part became a truly tiny one.

Blessing or Curse?

Next came the role that would make Johnny famous. He was reluctant to sign on to a television show, but the producers of *21 Jump Street* finally convinced him. The show debuted in 1987 and was an instant hit, especially with teens. For the first time in his life, Johnny had money. He didn't have to worry where his next month's rent would come

IN FOCUS

Rock City Angels

After *Platoon* was released in 1985, Johnny thought about giving up on acting and going back to music. He was ready to join a group called Rock City Angels. The band was originally from Miami but had recently moved to Los Angeles. They were in need of a guitarist. Johnny was excited about joining the band, but the paycheck *21 Jump Street* offered him changed his mind. He quit the band to take the job.

The Rock City Angels signed a $6 million recording deal with Geffen Records shortly after Johnny left. They released one album with Geffen, which flopped.

On the *Jump Street* set: Depp *(left)* and co-star Peter DeLuise *(right)* played undercover police officers at a high school in the hit show *21 Jump Street.*

from. But the price was heavy. Johnny became a teen idol—a tag he never wanted.

He also had to work on a show that he truly disliked. He didn't agree with the idea of police working as spies in high schools. He didn't like his character, Tom Hanson, and he wasn't a fan of the network executives at Fox either. And some reports said that Johnny's castmates weren't too thrilled with the amount of attention he was getting. In short, it was a bad situation all around.

Regardless, fans were in love with Johnny. His face was on the cover of almost every teenage magazine. Girls screamed at the sight of him. But it was a role he didn't want. He intended to build a long-lasting career, not just be a flash in the pan. "I don't want to make a career of taking my shirt off," he said. "I don't fault TV stars who do teen magazines. They took a hold of their situations; took offers that gave them big money fast. But they were dead in two years. I don't want that."

ℹ️ Many actors try to turn their fame into music careers. Johnny didn't want that. He still loved to play music. But he said, "I don't want to be a little teen idol boy who goes out there and sings pretty boy songs and makes tons of money because twelve-year-olds buy the records because I'm on [TV]."

Despite all the attention, Johnny was lonely. The show filmed in Vancouver, British Columbia, Canada. Sherilyn Fenn was in Los Angeles working. She and Johnny had trouble maintaining a long-distance relationship. They eventually broke up. Johnny asked his mother (newly remarried) and childhood friend Sal Jenco to move to Vancouver to keep him company. He even got Jenco a recurring role on the show. In time, Johnny found a new romantic interest in actress Jennifer Grey. The couple was briefly engaged to be married, but the romance didn't last even a year.

As a second and third season of the show aired, its popularity continued to grow.

Jennifer and Johnny: Depp was briefly engaged to actress Jennifer Grey, shown here in 1987.

Unfortunately, so did Johnny's dissatisfaction with it. "I was this product," he later said. "Teen boy. Poster boy. All the stuff that I wasn't. But they [the studio] made me that. It was horribly uncomfortable."

Johnny felt that he was doing something he didn't believe in. The studio also asked him to film public service announcements. He was supposed to tell kids to stay in school or to stay off drugs. But he had dropped out of school and used drugs and alcohol. He would feel like a hypocrite lecturing kids against such things.

Unhappy actor: Depp wasn't happy starring in *21 Jump Street* and wasn't afraid to show it on the set or in public.

Johnny was locked into a contract, though. He couldn't just quit. So he did the only other thing he could think to do. He made himself so unpleasant to work with that the show's producers wouldn't want him around. He refused to do certain scenes and even entire shows. He was surly. He acted out in public, getting into fights and generally misbehaving.

The show's producers knew what was happening. So in the show's third season, Johnny was featured less and less. The show hired a new actor, Richard Grieco, to eventually take Johnny's place as a new lead character, Booker. Johnny's days of playing Tom Hanson were nearing an end.

November 25, 1988

This 'Street' Is Jumping

<u>From the Pages of</u>
<u>USA TODAY</u>

VANCOUVER, British Columbia - The baby-faced cast of *21 Jump Street* is huddled outside a makeshift warehouse soundstage studying a parody of their hit show in the latest issue of the teen-oriented *Cracked* magazine.

Their Fox network show, which follows the travails (problems) of a team of undercover cops who pose as teenagers and fight youth crime, has become a darling among the younger generation and *Cracked* is the latest publication examining the show and its characters.

"Kids have discovered this show," says new executive producer Steve Beers, "and I think that sense of discovery has made it a kind of 'in' thing to watch."

Many cite the show's award-winning scripts, tackling such issues as AIDS, drinking and driving, child abuse, sexual molestation, drug abuse, date rape, prejudice and gay rights, as the main attraction.

But others cite the young cast—particularly heartthrob Johnny Depp, 25, who plays Officer Tom Hanson—as the real attraction.

Among girls, the slightly built actor "currently holds the pole position in budding fantasies all over America," writes *Rolling Stone* magazine.

Jump Street is an ensemble cast show with an asterisk—Depp. He is really the star, his character having been featured substantially more than the others.

"It's all right," says Peter DeLuise, who plays Officer Doug Penhall. "We all knew right from the start what we were getting into."

Although Beers as well as Fox executives deny it, the cast sees change looming.

"Something's happening," Depp says.

Depp, DeLuise and Dustin Nguyen claim some recent scripts have not been as good as those in the first two seasons. Although most cast members already get little screen time, a new actor was added and given plenty to do in the season opener.

The new regular is Richard Grieco, a darkly handsome former model playing rebellious Officer Dennis Booker.

The cast: The *21 Jump Street* cast got a new member in 1988—Richard Grieco. *From left to right*: Holly Robinson, Dustin Nguyen, Grieco, Peter DeLuise, Steven Williams, and Depp.

"It's obvious, isn't it?" DeLuise says. "This guy has been brought in as insurance in case Johnny leaves."

"We're not thinking of Grieco as a replacement," says Kevin Wendle, Fox executive vice president of Entertainment. "We brought him in to creatively stir up the ensemble and bring some new dramatic tension. It's working."

Depp has signed to do the show for three more seasons, Fox says. But the actor, who starred in the original *A Nightmare on Elm Street*, is clearly hot and wants to do movies.

—Tom Green

Breaking Free

As Johnny looked for ways to alienate himself from *21 Jump Street*, he also focused on resuming his film career. But Johnny found that most of the roles he was offered were similar to the character of Tom Hanson. He was being typecast. He knew that his career was at a crossroads. Producers were seeing him in a certain light, and he had to change that perception.

On the set: Director John Waters *(left)* cast Depp as the star of his film *Cry-Baby* (1990). Depp wanted to be in a movie that was very different from his role on *21 Jump Street*.

In 1989 Johnny read the script for a musical comedy titled *Cry-Baby*. Johnny knew he had found his chance to change the way people thought about him. Director John Waters offered him the role of Wade "Cry-Baby" Walker. Walker was a juvenile delinquent who fell in love with a rich girl. The beauty for Johnny was that *Cry-Baby* was a spoof of teenage romances. The film would give him the chance to make fun of all the brooding, misunderstood youths that directors thought Johnny should play.

The film enjoyed critical success, but it was far from a box-office hit. Still, it served Johnny's purposes. *Cry-Baby* announced to Hollywood that Johnny was more than just a teen idol.

Meanwhile, Johnny's personal life was changing as well. He had met an up-and-coming actress named Winona Ryder. Ryder was nineteen years old—eight years younger than Johnny—but that didn't stop

New girlfriend: Depp *(right)* and actress Winona Ryder *(left)* started dating in 1989. They are shown here at the premiere of Depp's movie *Cry-Baby* in 1990.

them from falling in love. Soon they became one of Hollywood's hottest couples. Tabloids followed their every move. The couple could barely step foot outside without a dozen cameras snapping photographs of them.

"When I met Winona and we fell in love, it was absolutely like nothing before," Johnny said at the time. "We hung out the whole day... and we've been hanging out ever since. I love her more than anything in the whole world."

Johnny, always quick to act on his emotions, proposed after just a few months. Once again, he was engaged. A humorous bumper sticker poked fun at Johnny's romantic history. It read "Honk if you've never been engaged to Johnny Depp." But this time, Johnny was convinced that the relationship would last.

And the good news kept coming. Johnny's agent had found a loophole in his contract for *21 Jump Street*. It allowed Johnny to break the contract and finally free himself from the show. Johnny was ready to take a big step forward in his career.

USA TODAY

CHAPTER THREE

Changing his image: Depp, shown here in 1989, wanted to be known as a serious, versatile actor.

The Next Phase

Johnny wasn't planning to pursue a typical Hollywood career. He didn't care much about stardom. He was far more concerned about working on interesting projects with interesting characters. Of course, even after *Cry-Baby*, most movie fans still equated Johnny with his former television character. They didn't see him as a serious actor. To many, he was just another Hollywood pretty boy. Johnny was ready to change their minds, in a big way.

Director Tim Burton had earned a reputation for making somewhat quirky, highly stylized (visually unique) films. Burton's latest project was a modern-day fairy tale called *Edward Scissorhands*. The title character is an artificially made man with the unlikely curse of having scissors for hands. It is a very loose interpretation of the old Frankenstein story.

Unique vision: Director Tim Burton *(above)* is known for his quirky, often darkly humorous movies.

Burton was torn as he tried to cast the role of Edward. The studio wanted Tom Cruise, but Burton did not think the young star was right for the role. He considered Tom Hanks, Robert Downey Jr., and even pop star Michael Jackson. Many of the top leading men in Hollywood were eager to play the part. But none of them quite matched Burton's vision. Burton just couldn't find the right actor. Then he met with Johnny Depp.

Johnny wanted the role. He identified with Edward, having often felt like an outcast himself. He just wasn't sure he could convince Burton that he could pull it off. "I was a TV boy," Johnny later said. "No director in his right mind would hire me to play this character. I had done nothing workwise to show I could handle this kind of role. How could I convince the director that I was Edward, that I knew him inside out?"

Johnny met with Burton and then waited. Weeks passed. Johnny continued to research the part. He became fixated on the film and on Edward. He later admitted that he didn't just want the part, he *needed it.*

Little did Johnny know, but he had nothing to worry about. Burton knew from the moment he met Johnny that he'd found his Edward. Burton was under pressure from the studio to hire a big-name movie star for the role. But Burton insisted on Johnny. It was a risk, but Burton was convinced. He finally called Johnny and offered him the part. Johnny wasted no time in accepting. And to top things off, Burton gave the female lead role to Winona Ryder (with whom he had worked on the 1988 movie *Beetlejuice*). Ryder was cast as Kim, Edward's love interest.

Hair, makeup, wardrobe: Depp and Ryder act in a scene from *Edward Scissorhands* (1990). They were a couple on- and offscreen.

Winona Ryder

Winona Ryder was born Winona Laura Horowitz in 1971. Her parents named her for the city of her birth—Winona, Minnesota. At age seven, Winona's family moved to a commune (shared property) in California. The Horowitzes lived on a plot of land with seven other families. They had no television or even electricity. Later, the family moved to a modern home in Petaluma, California.

Winona took an interest in acting at about age ten. She took acting lessons at the American Conservatory Theater in San Francisco. In 1985 she landed her first film role in *Lucas*. She asked to be credited as Winona Ryder. She chose that last name because her father had been recently listening to an album by musician Mitch Ryder.

Three years later, Ryder got the role that made her a star. She played Lydia Deetz in Tim Burton's *Beetlejuice*. She soon began dating Johnny, and the film roles kept coming. Her films of the 1990s included *Dracula*, *Little Women* (which earned her an Academy Award nomination), *Alien Resurrection*, and *Girl, Interrupted* (which she produced).

In 2001 Ryder made headlines when she was arrested for shoplifting. In the 2000s, Ryder's star faded somewhat. But she still found regular work acting. Her films of the decade included *Zoolander*, *Mr. Deeds*, and *Star Trek*.

Beetlejuice: Winona Ryder first worked with Tim Burton on the film *Beetlejuice*, released in 1988.

"Like Edward, Johnny really is perceived as something he's not," Burton said. "Before we met, I'd certainly read about him as the Difficult Heart-throb. But you look at him and you get a feeling. There's a lot of pain and humor and darkness and light. It's just a very strong internal feeling of loneliness. It's not something he talks about or even can talk about, because it's sad."

The role was demanding in many ways. Johnny spent hours each day in wardrobe and makeup. He had to wear a leather bodysuit even though the movie was filmed in the Florida heat. But it was all worthwhile. When it was released in December 1990, it instantly garnered critical acclaim. Johnny earned a Golden Globe nomination for Best Performance by an Actor in a Motion Picture—Comedy or Musical. The strange little story about a man with scissors for hands raked in more than $50 million at the box office.

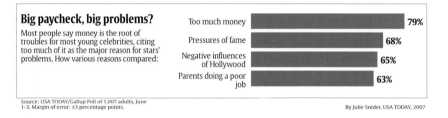

Big paycheck, big problems?

Most people say money is the root of troubles for most young celebrities, citing too much of it as the major reason for stars' problems. How various reasons compared:

Too much money	79%
Pressures of fame	68%
Negative influences of Hollywood	65%
Parents doing a poor job	63%

Source: USA TODAY/Gallup Poll of 1,007 adults, June 1-3. Margin of error: ±3 percentage points.

By Julie Snider, USA TODAY, 2007

The press wouldn't leave Johnny and Ryder alone. Ryder later said that the media pressure contributed to their breakup. "I remember us desperately hating being hounded [by the media]. It was horrible and it definitely took its toll on our relationship. Every day we heard that we were either cheating on each other or were broken up when we weren't. It was like this constant mosquito buzzing around us."

Twenty-seven-year-old Johnny had successfully left behind his reputation as a teen idol. There was no longer any doubt that he was a serious actor. His days of struggling to find good roles were over.

Professional Highs

Johnny's life changed rapidly with the release of *Edward Scissorhands*. He and Winona broke up, got back together, and broke up again. For three years, their on-again, off-again relationship was at the center of Hollywood gossip. The couple eventually split for good. According to those close to Johnny, he was devastated by the breakup.

Meanwhile, Johnny had a lot going on professionally. He accepted roles in several films (including a very small role in *Freddy's Dead: The Final Nightmare*, one of many sequels to *A Nightmare on Elm Street*). In 1993 he was featured in three films. In *Arizona Dream*, he plays a young man involved in a strange love triangle. The movie impressed some critics but was largely ignored by the public. *Benny & Joon* featured Johnny as Sam, an odd man who comes to stay with a brother and

Quirky character: Depp *(left)* and Mary Stuart Masterson *(right)* starred in the critically praised film *Benny & Joon* (1993).

sister, Benny and Joon. Once again, critics loved the film and Johnny's performance. But some commented that Johnny seemed to be trying too hard to find quirky roles in quirky films.

What's Eating Gilbert Grape was Johnny's third 1993 film. It featured Johnny as the title character. Gilbert is a young man in a small town struggling to cope with a family that includes a mentally challenged brother and a morbidly obese mother. According to many movie fans and critics, Johnny was nothing short of brilliant in the role.

"The special quality of What's Eating Gilbert Grape is not its oddness, . . . but its warmth," wrote legendary film critic Roger Ebert in the Chicago Sun-Times. "Johnny Depp, as Gilbert, has specialized in playing outsiders, and here he brings a quiet, gentle sweetness that suffuses the whole film."

Costars: Depp (center) starred in What's Eating Gilbert Grape (1993), along with Leonardo DiCaprio (left) and Juliette Lewis (right). DiCaprio received an Academy Award nomination for Best Supporting Actor for his role.

Johnny was generally liked and respected by his fellow actors. Leonardo DiCaprio, who received an Academy Award nomination for his role in *What's Eating Gilbert Grape*, spoke about his perception of Johnny. "There's an element of Johnny that is extremely nice and extremely cool," DiCaprio said. "But at the same time he's hard to figure out. But that makes him interesting."

Ebert spoke for the majority. But some viewed Johnny differently. Dan Yakir of *Sky* magazine wrote, "Depp's avoided one kind of stereotyping, but he faces the opposite danger; will he still be playing kooks when he's 40?"

Personal Lows

Johnny's film career was progressing rapidly. His personal life, however, was more complicated. In 1993 Johnny had helped to form a new band called P. Johnny played guitar and bass for the band, which also featured Flea of the Red Hot Chili Peppers. Later that year, Johnny bought a partial interest in a nightclub called the Viper Room. The club is in West Hollywood, a city in the Los Angeles area.

On the night of October 30, Johnny and the band were onstage at the Viper Room. River Phoenix, an actor and a friend of the band, was at the show. According to reports, Phoenix took drugs in the club's bathroom. In the very early hours of the morning of October 31, the young star overdosed on a mixture of cocaine and heroine. He died on the sidewalk in front of the Viper Room.

Johnny fell under intense criticism. People blamed him for the death. They said he was running a club that encouraged reckless drug use. He refused to answer his critics. He did feel a sense of responsibility

Tragic death: Actor River Phoenix *(above)* was outside Depp's West Hollywood club, the Viper Room, when he died of a drug overdose in 1993.

for Phoenix's death. And he did not want to contribute to what he saw as a media circus surrounding the tragedy.

Phoenix's death was just one factor that left Johnny increasingly unhappy with his personal life. His behavior was becoming erratic. Early in 1994,

USA TODAY Snapshots®

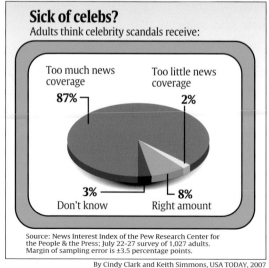

Sick of celebs?
Adults think celebrity scandals receive:

Too much news coverage
87%

Too little news coverage
2%

3%
Don't know

8%
Right amount

Source: News Interest Index of the Pew Research Center for the People & the Press; July 22-27 survey of 1,027 adults. Margin of sampling error is ±3.5 percentage points.

By Cindy Clark and Keith Simmons, USA TODAY, 2007

he was invited to the Academy Awards ceremony, where his job was to introduce music legend Neil Young. For someone who made his living in front of a camera, it should have been a simple task. But Johnny walked onto the stage and panicked. He was supposed to read lines from a teleprompter, but for some reason, he couldn't manage that. Instead, he blurted out a quick and clumsy introduction and rushed off the stage.

Reports also surfaced that Johnny was hurting himself. He was cutting his own skin, a behavior called self-mutilation. Johnny later compared the cuts to getting tattoos, but clearly this was a dark time in his life. He was using drugs more and more often. He wasn't eating or sleeping enough. His heart was racing. Once, friends had to rush him to the hospital, where doctors slowed his heartbeat.

In 1994 Johnny started dating twenty-year-old supermodel Kate Moss. One night, the couple was at a New York City hotel. Neighboring guests heard loud crashes from the couple's room. Johnny had trashed the room, breaking furniture and shattering glass. The police came, arrested Johnny, and led him away in handcuffs. He

Supermodel: Kate Moss *(left)* and Depp started dating in 1994. That same year, he was arrested after trashing a hotel room in New York City.

www.usatoday.com

USA TODAY

Life

SECTION D

December 14, 1993

Johnny Depp's down time /
What's eating the 'Grape' star

<u>From the Pages of</u>
<u>USA TODAY</u>

LOS ANGELES - Johnny Depp and River Phoenix weren't close friends. But they were on the same career track, doing films they believed in passionately but were rarely conventional.

"He was one of the actors in this town doing exactly what he wanted to do," says Depp, 30, co-owner of the Sunset Strip club where Phoenix, 23, died Oct. 31.

Depp has been trying to concentrate on his latest project, *What's Eating Gilbert Grape*, which opens Friday, but Phoenix's drug-related death has made it hard.

"There's a tragic loss of a very gifted, very sweet, nice young man," he says. But the media has been "disrespectful to River's loved ones." He cites repeated airings of the 911 call in which Phoenix's brother asked for help.

spent two days in jail. Rumors swirled about Johnny's violent outburst after a fight with Moss.

Johnny realized that he was making news for all the wrong reasons. It was time to refocus on his film career.

Choosing His Own Path

For good or bad, Johnny was a big name in Hollywood. Directors and producers wanted him in their films. Over the next several years, Johnny had opportunities to take on major roles in several blockbuster films. He was offered the part of Lestat in *Interview with the Vampire*.

He says his club, The Viper Room, is being slandered because of speculation about drug use there. "These reporters are playing backyard detective . . . turning it into some kind of sideshow. They're making accusations that just aren't true."

Depp says he is being grilled about drug use among young actors. "I just wonder where these people have been? I mean, do they think this is new? People overdose on drugs in Utah and Florida and New York City and all over the world. To pinpoint one club or one street is really ridiculous."

The club has reopened. There has been no police pressure to close, Depp says. The crowd of the curious has thinned, and it's back to the regulars.

Phoenix fans had written messages on the club doors in the days following his death, and the doors have been sent to EarthSave, a charity organization that Phoenix worked with. So were the flowers, candles and notes left outside.

Depp hasn't even seen *Gilbert*, in which he plays a grocery store clerk running out of chances for a life of his own because of a family that includes a 500-pound (227 kilogram) mother and a retarded brother.

He tends not to see his movies because "I freak out—why put yourself through something uncomfortable?"

The shoot came at a difficult time for Depp. His long romance with Winona Ryder was ending. "It was sort of an in-and-out thing with us, very up and down." But director Lasse Hallström (*My Life as a Dog*) sensed his feelings and helped him do the emotional role.

Depp made his depression work. "Whatever I was feeling, it was close to the surface, so it was easy to manipulate."

—Tom Green

But he turned it down, and the role went to Tom Cruise. He also declined the role of Tristan in *Legends of the Fall*, which went to Brad Pitt. He even had a chance to star in the action film *Speed*, but he let that role go to Keanu Reeves.

The truth was that Johnny wasn't interested in making blockbusters. His only motivation was to make the movies that excited him. If they could gain some widespread popularity, all the better.

Johnny's next project reunited him with Burton. Johnny played the title character in *Ed Wood* (1994), a biopic (biographical film) about a 1950s movie director. Ed Wood was famous for making some of the

Johnny as Ed: In 1994 Depp *(right)* took the title role in *Ed Wood*, a Tim Burton film about a failed movie director.

worst movies of all time. In the decades since his 1978 death, Wood's name had become something of a punch line among film fans. But Johnny—known for making some strange film choices himself—felt a sort of kinship with the much-maligned director.

"Ed was someone who was not afraid to take chances and did exactly what he wanted to do," Johnny said. "He did the best he could do with what was available to him. . . . His movies were all his and they were genuine."

The film didn't do well at the box office. But it did gain a cult following and earned rave reviews from critics. The Internet Movie Database (IMDb.com), an Internet site that collects user ratings for all films, has it ranked among the top 200 films of all time. Johnny earned yet another Golden Globe nomination and further cemented himself as one of Hollywood's brightest stars.

Ed Wood

Ed Wood, born in New York in 1924, was fascinated by storytelling. After serving in World War II (1939–1945), he returned to the United States and followed his dream of writing and making films. His first major film was 1953's *Glen or Glenda*. The movie's title character is a man who secretly dresses in women's clothing.

Wood went on to write, produce, and direct many more movies over the next decade. He often wrote his own scripts. He usually had little or no budget, and the lack of production value showed. His most famous film was probably *Plan 9 from Outer Space* (1959). As many of his films did, it featured aging actor Bela Lugosi. The film remains, in the minds of many, the worst motion picture ever made. That status has actually kept it alive. It still plays on screens worldwide, but mostly so audiences can make fun of it as they watch.

Wood's career spiraled downward in the 1960s. He died in 1978, generally forgotten by the public. Two years later, the book *The*

Wood's plan: Wood's *Plan 9 from Outer Space* is often considered one of the worst movies ever made.

Golden Turkey Awards named him the worst director of all time. The "award" brought Wood's name into the limelight, and suddenly it was fashionable to make fun of him and his movies.

Seven months after the 1994 release of *Ed Wood*, Johnny bought a $2.3 million mansion in Hollywood. The mansion had once belonged to actor Bela Lugosi, famous for starring in horror movies in the 1930s and 1940s. Lugosi (played by Martin Landau) also figured as an important character in *Ed Wood*. Johnny loved the home's history and interesting architecture.

Home with history: In 1995 Depp bought the home of movie actor Bela Lugosi in California's Hollywood Hills.

On-screen with a legend: Depp *(right)* costarred with acting legend Marlon Brando *(left)* in *Don Juan DeMarco* (1995). The movie failed at the box office.

But even Johnny's reputation couldn't turn his next several films into successes. *Don Juan DeMarco*, *Dead Man*, and *Nick of Time* were all released in 1995. And all were critical and commercial disappointments. In *Don Juan DeMarco*, Johnny played the title character—a man who considered himself the world's greatest lover. In *Dead Man*, his role was that of William Blake, a murderer on the run. *Nick of Time* is a thriller featuring Johnny as the father of a kidnapped daughter. Johnny got some favorable reviews for his performances, but for the most part, the public ignored all three films. Johnny needed another breakout role to remind moviegoers of what made him so special.

Actor, director, writer: Depp, shown here in 1995, tried something new with his next movie, *The Brave*. He not only acted in the film, but he directed it and cowrote the screenplay.

Brave Choices

Johnny was ready to try something new in his career. He threw himself into a new project, *The Brave*. The film was based on a novel of the same name by Gregory McDonald. It told the story of a Native American man, Raphael, struggling to provide for his family. It is a dark story about a man having to make a terrible choice, and it touched Johnny deeply. Johnny had helped co-write the screenplay. He was also ready to try his hand as a director.

The budget for *The Brave* was small. Acting legend Marlon Brando agreed to a small role in the film. But Johnny found that he couldn't afford to hire a lead actor. So he decided to play the part himself. Johnny found that serving as the director and as the star was demanding. He'd direct and act all day in the extreme desert heat of Death Valley, California. Then at night, he'd prepare for the next day's shooting. "I thought I was going to die, every day," Johnny said. "I would shoot all day and act as well, then go home, do rewrites, do my homework as an actor; do my homework as a director. Go to sleep and even then I'd dream about the film. It was a nightmare."

The grueling schedule left little time for a personal life. His relationship with Moss suffered, and the pair split. Worse still, Johnny was so rushed that he didn't have time to properly edit the film's ending. Regardless, he was proud of what he'd accomplished.

Filming *The Brave*: Depp reviews film of a scene from *The Brave* (1996) with a young costar and other members of the film crew.

The Brave debuted at the popular Cannes Film Festival in France in 1997. Johnny was nervous as the film played. When it finished, part of the audience gave it a standing ovation. Some people were even in tears. Johnny must have believed the film was a success. But the critics thought differently. "[The critics] just . . . destroyed us," Johnny said. "It was like an attack on me—how dare I direct a movie? They ate me alive. It was vicious. I was totally, totally shocked."

 The Brave was never released in U.S. theaters, largely due to the harsh criticism it suffered after the Cannes Film Festival. Johnny later reedited the film and released it in the United States on DVD.

Donnie Brasco

Johnny had signed on to do a movie titled *Divine Rapture*. He traveled to Ireland, where filming began. But after a week, the filming halted. The film's financial backing had dried up. The movie was canceled.

The cancellation was a disappointment that hurt a lot of people financially. But Johnny already had bigger and brighter things on the horizon. He had signed on to play the lead in *Donnie Brasco*. The movie told the real-life story of Joe Pistone, an undercover FBI agent who infiltrated New York City organized crime in the 1970s. Pistone went by the name Donnie Brasco to help gather evidence to put Mafia crime bosses in prison.

Johnny's role was daunting. He researched it by spending time with actual members of the Mafia. He wanted to get a sense of how they behaved, spoke, and interacted. He knew that it was dangerous to rub elbows with such men, especially since he was playing the role of an informant and a real-life person detested by many members of the Mafia.

IN F⊕CUS

The Mafia

In *Donnie Brasco*, Johnny played an undercover agent infiltrating the Mafia. The Mafia is a name given to a large organized crime group that grew out of the Italian island of Sicily. Another name for the group is La Cosa Nostra.

The Mafia is made up of many small groups called families or clans. Each family holds power over a certain region, such as a city or a neighborhood, and is ruled by a boss called a don. The Mafia has traditionally been most powerful in Italy. But it has also enjoyed periods of significant power and influence in U.S. cities.

The Mafia has a reputation for dealing with informants and undercover agents very harshly. When Joe Pistone went undercover, his life was at risk every day. After he testified in a trial that sent Mafia leaders to prison, he knew he would never be safe again. He had to move to another state and live under an assumed name. Although the Mafia's power in America has dimmed, the organization still does exist.

In a way, the role allowed Johnny to come full circle on his acting career. His first big break had been as an undercover cop on *21 Jump Street*. He had hated that role and that character, but this was different. He had met and liked Pistone, and his was a character Depp could sympathize with.

"It's wrong to say that Joe was betraying [the Mafia]," Johnny explained in defense of his character. "If he had been a Mafia guy from the beginning and then turned on

Undercover: FBI agent Joe Pistone, shown here in 1997, infiltrated the Mafia in New York City in the 1970s.

February 27, 1997

Depp delves into the heart of mob life in 'Brasco'

From the Pages of
USA TODAY

Imagine pretending to be a mobster for six years. Imagine your life depending on how good an actor you are. No rehearsals, no second takes, no bad reviews. Just a bullet.

That's what was on Johnny Depp's mind as he played ex-FBI agent Joseph Pistone in *Donnie Brasco*, which opens Friday. The true story, drawn from Pistone's book, tells how he posed as a small-time jewel thief, Donnie Brasco, and penetrated the Bonanno crime family in the '70s.

"When I first read the book and met with Joe and spoke about his life and what he had been through, I was only able to understand to a certain extent," Depp says. "But when I heard the surveillance tapes, and I heard him speaking to these guys . . . then you really get the picture of what he had to go through, of what he was living with every day of his life."

Already Depp is getting raves for his career-turning Brasco role opposite mob film veteran Al Pacino as Lefty Ruggiero. Pacino himself played an undercover cop in *Serpico* (1973) when he was 33, Depp's age.

Brasco is less a mob shoot-'em-up than a character-driven story of loyalty and betrayal. Pacino plays the washed-up wise guy who becomes Brasco's mentor. It is the father-son relationship that develops between the two men that is the often tender heart of the film.

—Elizabeth Snead

his friends and associates, then that would have been a betrayal. But the fact is that Joe came in as an FBI agent and he was just doing his job. . . . He is maybe the strongest person I ever met in my life."

Pistone was equally impressed. "[Johnny] captured me to a tee," he said. "He absorbs so much. He doesn't try, it just comes to him. And he remembers everything. He's like a sponge. . . . He's a lovely guy."

Johnny's dedication—and his on-screen chemistry with costar Al Pacino—helped make the film a big success. Fans and critics loved it. Susan Wloszczyna of *USA Today* wrote, "Johnny Depp digs deep into the troubled soul of the agent who is torn between two families . . . and comes up with his most winning performance yet. Like Pacino's undercover cop in Serpico, it's all in the eyes. Depp's intense orbs focus like surveillance cameras, taking in each crime and confrontation. He's sucked into the brutal, bullying lifestyle, and so are we."

Gangster life: Al Pacino *(left)* costarred with Depp *(right)* in *Donnie Brasco* (1997). Pacino is famous for playing another Mafia role—Michael Corleone in *The Godfather* (1972) and its sequels.

New York Times film critic Janet Maslin agreed. "Mr. Depp's tremendous talent is no longer surprising," she wrote. "With this film [*Donnie Brasco*] his career reaches critical mass, turning an assortment of varied, offbeat roles into the trajectory of a major star."

A Strange Trip

Several years earlier, Johnny had, by chance, met author Hunter S. Thompson. Thompson had written the novel *Fear and Loathing in Las Vegas*, which Johnny had read and loved as a teenager. During the filming of *Donnie Brasco*, Thompson had called Johnny. The book, which recounted some of Thompson's drug-induced experiences, was in the early stages of being turned into a film. Thompson wanted Johnny to play the lead role.

Johnny jumped at the chance. He joined Thompson on a book tour and got to know him better. The author was famously eccentric (some might call him downright strange), and Johnny was determined to portray him accurately. After the book tour, Johnny actually moved in with Thompson and slept on his couch. He studied the man for four months and even drove Thompson's car from Los Angeles to Las Vegas, where filming would begin.

"I felt under tremendous pressure," Johnny said. "I was so freaked out by the idea of disappointing Hunter. So I did my best to absorb him. My goal was to steal his soul. That's what I wanted to do, to try and take as much of him as possible and put him into my body."

The end result was a love-it-or-hate-it affair. The film is highly stylized and crafted to put the audience into the minds of the characters, most of whom are on drugs. Some moviegoers found the film to be a truly unique piece of art. Many others found it confusing, disorienting, and all but impossible to follow. The film's seemingly pro-drug stance put Johnny under the microscope once again. He had long been accused of being a drug abuser, and his convincing portrayal in *Fear and Loathing in Las Vegas* only furthered that belief.

In-depth study: Depp *(left)* and Hunter S. Thompson *(right)* pose at the 1998 movie premiere of *Fear and Loathing in Las Vegas*. Depp spent a lot of time with Thompson before playing him in the film.

For his part, Johnny insisted that the movie was not pro-drugs. He claimed that the confusing experiences of the characters would convince anyone to stay away from drugs. "I mean, come on, this is like a drug nightmare," he said. "What were people expecting? *Peter Pan*? This is *Fear and Loathing*."

Many felt his words rang hollow. But few could deny that Johnny had provided audiences with an authentic, one-of-a-kind performance.

Big Changes

Johnny's personal life remained in the news. In 1998 he was spotted with Moss on several occasions, sparking rumors that the couple had reunited. (They insisted they were together just as friends.)

Johnny's next role wasn't anything like his previous choices. He signed on to play Spencer Armacost in *The Astronaut's Wife*. Spencer is a husband, father, and astronaut. During one of his space shuttle missions, the spacecraft loses radio contact with Earth for two minutes. Spencer returns to Earth, but his behavior has changed. His wife becomes convinced that something terrible happened to him in space.

Cannes: *(Left to right)* Kate Moss, Depp, and actor Benicio Del Toro attend the Cannes Film Festival in France in 1998. *Fear and Loathing in Las Vegas* was up for an award at the festival.

Close observation: Depp starred as a book dealer in *The Ninth Gate*, a 1999 film by director Roman Polanski.

The film allowed Johnny to show some new sides to himself, although audiences generally found the film forgettable.

The same could be said for 1999's *The Ninth Gate*. The film was intended to be a blockbuster. But it had a confusing plot about a book dealer searching for texts rumored to have a connection to the devil. It failed to inspire both critics and the moviegoing public.

The Ninth Gate did little for Johnny's career. But it did change his life forever. Johnny's days as a carefree young man with few personal responsibilities were coming to an end.

City of love: Depp was in Paris, France (*above*), filming *The Ninth Gate* when he got reacquainted with French actress Vanessa Paradis. The relationship would mean big changes for the actor.

Family Man

Johnny was in Paris, France, while filming *The Ninth Gate*. One night at a hotel bar, he spotted actress and model Vanessa Paradis. The two had met before, but one or the other had always been involved in a relationship. This time, both of them were single. Johnny asked Paradis to join him at his table, and the two hit it off.

Within a few months, the couple was living together in Paris. After a few more months, Paradis told Johnny that he was going to be a father.

The pregnancy was good news. The bad news was that Johnny had to deal with even more attention from the media. Paparazzi (photographers who take pictures of celebrities in public) hounded the high-profile couple. Tabloids spread rumors about them. One rumor said that Johnny was cheating on Paradis with pop star Madonna. One night, Johnny snapped. He and Paradis were leaving a restaurant. Paparazzi surrounded the couple, snapping photographs. Johnny asked them to leave, but they only got more aggressive. Johnny was irate. He pushed a camera into one photographer, cutting the man's face. Then Johnny picked up a piece of wood and threatened to hit the photographers with it. Someone called the police, and Johnny was arrested. The injured photographer declined to press charges, however, and Johnny was soon released.

French love: Depp's new love interest, Vanessa Paradis *(above)*, is a well-known singer, model, and actress in France. She had her first hit song at fourteen.

Box-Office Smash

Johnny's next film was a true blockbuster. He took on the role of Ichabod Crane in *Sleepy Hollow*, a retelling of Washington Irving's classic 1820 tale *The Legend of Sleepy Hollow*. In the movie version, Crane is a timid detective out to investigate stories of a ghostly headless horseman. The film reunited Johnny with director Tim Burton, with whom he'd enjoyed so much success on *Ed Wood* and *Edward Scissorhands*.

Johnny played opposite his close friend Christina Ricci. The press saw the two together off-camera, and instantly rumors flew that they were having an affair. With Paradis at home in Paris and pregnant, the tabloids seemed determined to stir things up. Johnny dismissed the rumors. He said that he thought of Ricci almost as a little sister. Even the pair's romantic scenes in the movie, he said, made him uncomfortable.

The 1999 film was a smash hit. It took in more than $100 million at the box office—by far Johnny's most profitable movie to date. Burton

Friends and coworkers: Depp *(left)* worked with good friend Christina Ricci *(right)* in the Tim Burton movie *Sleepy Hollow* (1999). Ricci had also appeared with Depp in *Fear and Loathing in Las Vegas* (1998).

Click, Flash: Depp and Vanessa Paradis arrive at the premiere of *Sleepy Hollow* in 1999.

gave Depp a lot of credit for the movie's success. Johnny, he said, added a critical element of humor to Crane's character. The humor stood in contrast to the film's generally dark mood, creating an important contrast. Johnny's ability to mix a sense of humor with dark subject matter would prove to be a valuable asset later in his career.

Small Parts

On May 27, 1999, Paradis gave birth to a daughter. The couple couldn't decide between the names Lily and Rose, so they named her Lily-Rose Melody Depp. The middle name, Melody, came from the couple's shared love for music.

Johnny was thrilled with his new daughter. He was thirty-five years old and felt ready to start a family. But he was not thrilled that the couple had to sneak the baby out of the hospital to avoid a large group of paparazzi camped outside. Even as they returned to their Paris home, a helicopter hovered overhead, carrying a photographer hoping to snap the first photograph of Lily-Rose. Johnny had always held the paparazzi in contempt, but their pursuit of his infant daughter enraged him.

After Lily-Rose was born, Johnny and Paradis were slated to appear together in the movie *The Man Who Killed Don Quixote.* But the film was canceled after just five days of shooting.

Johnny and Paradis decided to live in Paris full time. They felt France offered them more privacy than they could find in California. There, Johnny teamed up with fellow actors Sean Penn, John Malkovich, and others to open his own restaurant, Man Ray. The restaurant was a hit. The Viper Room was also still open and doing well.

After Lily-Rose's birth, Johnny decided to work less. "Vanessa and I agreed never to work simultaneously," he said. "So small parts that allowed me not to be away for long were welcome. Evidently, the rumor spread and all at once there were a lot of small parts."

Home sweet home: Depp and Paradis lived with their daughter in the south of France in the early 2000s. Depp liked that his family could live in relative privacy in the country.

November 29, 1999

Character roles save Depp from hollow stardom

From the Pages of
USA TODAY

LOS ANGELES—In faded flannel shirt, weathered jeans, scuffed boots and a leather wristband, with his long hair struggling under a knit cap, Johnny Depp looks more like a starving . . . artist than a Hollywood movie star.

Especially when his welcoming grin reveals two gold teeth.

"I had them done in this really bad gold," Depp says proudly of the period dental decor he came up with for the part of a Gypsy hiding in Nazi-occupied Paris for *The Man Who Cried*, which just finished shooting.

Depp, who stars as persnickety police inspector Ichabod Crane in *Sleepy Hollow*, clearly has a blast transforming his handsome self into some strange cinematic characters.

"'Movie star' never applied to me," he says. "I never felt I could be that. I always wanted to be a character actor. I take roles because I fall in love with the character. And I jump at the chance to do roles that will only come around once."

That's what drew him to the unfinished, kindhearted freak in *Edward Scissorhands*, the shy outcast in *What's Eating Gilbert Grape* (he had his teeth bonded and chipped for the role), the brash New York [Mafia] informer in *Donnie Brasco*, the balding, drugged-out Hunter S. Thompson alter ego in *Fear and Loathing in Las Vegas*, even the obsessive Latin lover in *Don Juan deMarco*.

He's still at it. Depp's upcoming film roles are just as quirky. He plays an unscrupulous rare-books investigator in Roman Polanski's demonic mystery *The Ninth Gate*.

"People say I make strange choices, but they're not strange to me," Depp says. "My sickness is that I am fascinated by human behavior, by what's underneath the surface, by the worlds inside people."

—Elizabeth Snead

Over the next year, Johnny took on several such roles. He made an appearance in the final episode of the French TV program *The Fast Show*. He made a cameo (small, unpublicized) appearance in the 2000 World War II drama *The Man Who Cried*, in which he plays a mysterious gypsy.

Johnny also took minor roles in the Julian Schnabel film *Before Night Falls*. The film is about a homosexual man from Cuba. Johnny played the parts of two gay men, Lieutenant Victor and Bon Bon. Even in small roles, Johnny made a big impression on the film's star, Javier Bardem.

"I think [Johnny] did amazing work and he was very generous, very helpful," Bardem said. "He really got into the mood of the character, Bon Bon, and that scene with him as Lieutenant Victor is something that will stay in my memory. I admire him a great deal, as an actor and a human being."

Sweet and Sour

Johnny was enjoying this pattern of small roles that didn't demand too much of his time. So next, he agreed to appear in Lasse Hallström's *Chocolat*. The film is about a chocolate shop in a French village in the

Music and motion pictures: In *Chocolat* (2000), Depp *(right)* had a supporting role opposite French actress Juliette Binoche *(left)*. Depp played guitar in the movie.

In *Chocolat*, Johnny's character ate chocolate in many scenes. As the crew filmed the scenes again and again, Johnny had to keep eating. By the time he was done, he said he couldn't stand the sight of chocolate anymore.

1950s. The shop owner serves up treats with the power to affect people's emotions. Johnny played Roux, a free-spirited traveler. The role called for Johnny to do something he'd never had a chance to do on film before—play his guitar.

Chocolat was a critical success. It was nominated for the 2001 Academy Award for Best Picture. Johnny also got a personal honor about the same time—his own star on the famous Hollywood Walk of Fame.

Family moment: Depp was surrounded by family when he received a star on the Hollywood Walk of Fame in 1999. *Left to right:* Depp's father, John Depp; mother, Betty Sue Depp; girlfriend, Vanessa Paradis; Depp; and sisters Deborah Depp and Christie Dembrowski.

Johnny wanted to bring six-month-old Lily-Rose to Hollywood with him for the unveiling of his star. But in the end, he decided against it. He had come to distrust Hollywood—most specifically the press there. The constant hounding he'd suffered since emerging as a star in the late 1980s had badly soured him on the media, Hollywood, and even on the United States in general. He believed that Lily-Rose deserved her privacy. It wasn't her fault, he reasoned, that she'd been born to famous parents.

Johnny's disgust at his treatment in the United States was no secret. Nor was his distaste for its political leadership, especially the policies of President George W. Bush. "The life we lead now [in France] looks like a normal life, as far as that is possible in our profession," he said. "I don't hate America; I nurse a beautiful feeling for what it once was or could have been—people in the Midwest who simply work and try to survive. But I hate the ambitions, the short-sightedness, the needless pain and violence in families. I feel an aversion to what America has become. I almost became crazy there myself. I certainly won't expose my girl to it."

Some fans were offended by Johnny's commentary. Many viewed him as an elitist (a person who thinks of himself or herself as being superior to others). Others dismissed him as just another ultraliberal celebrity. But for Johnny, the issue was the quality of life he could provide Lily-Rose. He didn't care what people thought. He believed that France was the best place for his daughter to grow up.

Return to the Lead

Johnny had enjoyed his time playing small roles and cameos. But it was time for him to return to leading roles. First came 2001's *Blow*, a film about real-life drug smuggler George Jung. Johnny took the role of Jung. In the late 1970s and early 1980s, Jung was a large-scale drug trafficker, smuggling cocaine into the United States from South America.

It was a challenging role. Johnny had to portray Jung over a period

Blow by blow: Depp *(left)* and director Ted Demme *(right)* discuss a scene while filming the 2001 movie *Blow*. Depp played drug smuggler George Jung.

of more than a decade, showing the man's many sides and complex personality. Johnny read Jung's autobiography and visited him in prison for two days. He studied Jung's mannerisms. He learned how Jung walked and talked. Jung reportedly was so moved by Johnny's portrayal of him that he was in tears through much of the film.

The film's director Ted Demme agreed. "[Johnny] never gives a dishonest take," he said. "From day one he became George Jung and the nuances he brought to the part never ceased to amaze me. His instincts are impeccable, not just as an actor but as a person."

Blow was a critical success and a moderate box-office hit, raking in more than $50 million. *USA Today* film critic Mike Clark called it, "one of the few major releases so far this year that is worth a grown-up's time."

Next up for Johnny was *From Hell*, a crime mystery set in London, England, in the 1880s. Johnny plays a police inspector trying to find Jack the Ripper. It was an exciting film for Johnny, who had always been fascinated by the famous killer. As a child, he had seen a documentary on the mystery and already knew a great deal about the case.

The film took in more than $30 million, but it drew lukewarm reviews. Many saw it as overly violent with an unsophisticated plot. Johnny, in particular, was criticized for his unconvincing and inconsistent Cockney (local London) accent.

Jack the Ripper: The front page of this 1888 British newspaper sensationalized the mysterious murderer known as Jack the Ripper.

If Johnny was unhappy about the reception of *From Hell*, he wouldn't have been for long. In late 2001, he and Paradis learned that she was once again pregnant. In June 2002, the couple welcomed a baby boy, Jack, into the family. Johnny took most of the year off to be with his young family. When he returned to film, it would be with a bang.

IN FOCUS

Jack the Ripper

Johnny jumped at the chance to appear in *From Hell* (2001). He had long been interested in history's most famous serial killer.

Jack the Ripper was the name given to the person who killed at least five people (and probably more) in London, England, in 1888. Jack the Ripper made headlines that year as he targeted women in London's poor neighborhoods. His crimes were very violent. The Ripper carefully removed internal organs from several victims. This led police to believe that the killer was possibly a doctor who knew a great deal about human anatomy.

Over several months, the unsolved murders became a media sensation. According to reports, the killer himself encouraged the coverage, going so far as to send a body part from one of the victims to a newspaper.

Investigators never determined Jack the Ripper's true identity. But people continued to be fascinated by the killer long after the murders stopped. More than a century later, people still study the case and develop theories about who the killer might have been.

CHAPTER SIX

Movie star dad: Depp, shown here in 2004, was a committed family man by the early 2000s. His choice of movies reflected his changing personal life.

Sailing to the Top

By 2003 thirty-nine-year-old Johnny was a well-respected leading man. He was admired by fans and peers alike for his honest portrayals of a wide range of characters. But he was by no means considered among Hollywood's true elite. He hadn't yet vaulted into that upper level inhabited by the likes of Tom Cruise, Tom Hanks, and Will Smith. That was about to change.

The change began with an unlikely choice. Now a father, Johnny had an interest in films his children could enjoy. So he signed on for the film *Finding Neverland*. He played J. M. Barrie, who wrote the 1904 play *Peter Pan* after being inspired by a young family he befriended. The character called for Johnny to speak in a Scottish accent, so he hired a voice coach to help him get it right. No doubt the criticism he got for his accent in *From Hell* contributed to this decision. By all accounts, his work paid off.

The film was originally to be titled *Neverland* and released in the summer

Peter Pan: Depp played author J. M. Barrie *(above)* in the 2004 film *Finding Neverland*. Barrie wrote the play *Peter Pan* in 1904.

of 2003. But a few months before the scheduled release date, an independent film bearing the same name was released. So Johnny's film was delayed and the title was changed to *J. M. Barrie's Neverland*. It was postponed again so as not to interfere with the release of yet

Academy Award nominee: Depp and Paradis attended the Oscars in 2005 when he was nominated for his role in *Finding Neverland*.

another movie, *Peter Pan*. Finally, with one last name change to *Finding Neverland*, the film was released in October 2004. It was a great success and won Johnny an Academy Award nomination.

The Role of a Lifetime

As a father, Johnny vowed to make different choices. He knew that many of his films hadn't been big moneymakers. When he was single, that had been fine. In fact, he had been proud of the fact that he was not willing to "sell out" by taking roles just for a big payday. But with two children to support, it was time to accept some roles in big-budget movies. And so when Disney contacted him about playing the lead in a movie based on their Pirates of the Caribbean theme park ride, Johnny agreed. The $14 million they offered him to play the role must have made the decision an easy one.

> Being a father changed Johnny's whole outlook on life. He explained what having a family meant to him. "It's only because of my family that I'm a better person and I'm much more centered than I've ever been. . . . My kids gave me life. They are the greatest thing that's ever happened."

The film, titled *Pirates of the Caribbean: The Curse of the Black Pearl*, was designed from the beginning to be a blockbuster. It was actually a big risk, both for Disney and for Johnny. In 1995 another big-budget pirate movie called *Cutthroat Island* had been a complete bomb at the box office. Some movie executives questioned whether the public really had an appetite for pirate movies. Still, Disney was convinced and backed the project with a budget of almost $150 million. For Johnny's part, he was risking a reputation he'd spent almost two decades building. If he was signing on for a big-budget film, it had better be a good one.

Johnny set to work studying pirates. His character, Captain Jack Sparrow, was a pirate seeking a cursed ghost ship called the *Black Pearl*. Johnny decided that pirates reminded him a little of modern-day rock stars. Specifically, Johnny began thinking about his friend Keith Richards, guitarist for the legendary band the Rolling Stones. "Pirates were the rock stars of their day," he said. "[Keith Richards] is

Pirate model: Keith Richards, guitarist for iconic rock band the Rolling Stones, was one of Depp's inspirations for the character Captain Jack Sparrow.

not far off being a pirate." Johnny began spending time with Richards, but he didn't reveal that he was studying the rocker's speech habits and mannerisms. Richards was not the only inspiration for Jack Sparrow, of course. Johnny also admitted to drawing upon the smooth-talking cartoon skunk Pepe Le Pew.

How would such a strange combination—rock star and cartoon skunk—come off on film? At first, Disney executives thought it might be a disaster. They felt that Johnny was playing the character all wrong, and one exec went so far as to say that Johnny was ruining the movie. Another wondered if Sparrow was supposed to be drunk. The movie honchos went so far as to ask Johnny to rein in his performance a bit.

Johnny explained to the executives that he didn't want to compromise the character. He even told them that if they didn't want him to play the part his way, they should just fire him. "They were really worried and, in a lot of ways, rightly so," he later said. "They had a lot of dough invested in the thing and here comes this really weird guy doing something they never experienced before from a human being. I did understand it, but it didn't change anything. I still had to do what I had to do, even when the threat was to potentially be fired."

Director Gore Verbinski stood by his star, and Johnny was allowed to play Sparrow the way he envisioned him. The Disney executives would eventually come around.

According to executive producer Mike Stenson, "In a 500-channel universe, where you have so many different opportunities to be entertained in so many ways, you have to give the audience something that's unique and different. That's exactly what Johnny did with Captain Jack Sparrow in *The Curse of the Black Pearl*. He created this character and had absolutely committed to it."

Captain Jack: Depp's portrayal of Captain Jack Sparrow in *The Curse of the Black Pearl* (2003) was initially a hard sell to movie executives.

Smash Hit

In hindsight, Disney's reluctance about Johnny's portrayal of Captain Jack Sparrow seems hard to believe. *Pirates of the Caribbean: The Curse of the Black Pearl* opened July 9, 2003, to massive crowds. The movie made $70 million in the first five days alone and went on to gross (take in from ticket sales) more than $650 million total worldwide. The film combined a good cast with lots of action and impressive special effects. But there was no doubt that Johnny was the main attraction. He was so convincing as Captain Jack that reportedly even his young daughter was confused. She believed that her father really was a pirate.

The critics received the film with mixed reviews. Some hated it, saying it was not believable or was too long. Others said it glorified eighteenth-century piracy—what was in truth a brutal, violent way of

Playing to the crowd: Depp talks to fans at a screening of *Pirates of the Caribbean: The Curse of the Black Pearl* in California in 2003. The movie was wildly popular with moviegoers when it was released that summer.

life. Many others loved it. *USA Today* film critic Claudia Puig called it "the summer blockbuster we've been waiting for."

Roger Ebert of the *Chicago Sun-Times* gave it mixed praise. He said the movie was too long and, at times, pointless. But he loved Johnny's performance. "Depp in particular seems to be channeling a drunken drag queen, with his eyeliner and the way he minces ashore and slurs his dialogue," Ebert wrote. "Don't mistake me: This is not a criticism, but admiration for his work. It can be said that his performance is original in its every atom. There has never been a pirate, or for that matter a human being, like this in any other movie."

The film was nominated for five Academy Awards. Among those was Johnny's nomination for Best Actor. Johnny was also nominated for a Golden Globe, won the MTV Movie Award for Best Actor, and won the Screen Actors Guild Award for Outstanding Performance by a Male Actor in a Leading Role. Any doubts that remained about Johnny's box-office appeal had been erased forever.

Dumb Puppy

The Curse of the Black Pearl put Johnny squarely among Hollywood's elite. Could he hope to maintain that level of excellence with his next performance?

Johnny was already hard at work filming *Once Upon a Time in Mexico*. The film was written as a sequel to the action movie *Desperado*. Johnny played Sands, a corrupt CIA (Central Intelligence Agency) agent. Sands is trying to help break up a plot to kill the president of Mexico.

Johnny had long wanted to work with director Robert Rodriguez and was intrigued by the character of Sands. Sands was unlike any role Johnny had played before. He was excited for a challenge. "[Sands] wasn't someone who was clichéd or who I felt I had seen before," Johnny explained. "He is a man who has no regard for human life. I've never played someone like that before, who's not a good guy in any way."

A villain: Depp arrives at the premiere of *Once Upon a Time in Mexico* at the Venice Film Festival in 2003. The movie, directed by Robert Rodriguez, featured Depp in a bad-guy role and did very well at the box office.

Could Johnny pull off the role of a true bad guy? Fans and critics agreed: Johnny nailed the part. "Depp tosses off nearly as many dead-pan quips as he did in *Pirates* and steals the movie from everyone else in the cast," wrote *USA Today*'s Claudia Puig.

The movie garnered critical acclaim and box-office success when it premiered in September 2003. Yet Johnny made headlines for a different reason. A German magazine printed quotes from Johnny in which he spoke out against the United States, particularly against President George W. Bush and his international policies.

"America is dumb," Johnny said. "It's like a dumb puppy that has big teeth that can bite and hurt you, aggressive. My daughter is four, my boy is one. I'd like them to see America as a toy, a broken toy. Investigate it a little, check it out, get this feeling and then get out."

Johnny was harshly criticized for his statements. He later backed off what he had said, trying to explain that he'd been quoted out of context. He claimed that he meant nothing more than that the United States wasn't as old as European countries. He said that he loved his country. Still, for some of his fans, the damage was done.

Minor Successes

After his over-the-top performance as Captain Jack Sparrow, Johnny was eager to find a more understated role. He found that in 2004's *Secret Window*, a thriller based on a novel by Stephen King. In it, Johnny plays Mort Rainey, a writer accused by a strange man of plagiarism (passing off another's work as one's own). Rainey is going through a divorce, and his life seems to be falling apart around him. The character is introspective, depressed, and about as far from Captain Jack Sparrow as Johnny could get.

David Koepp wrote the screenplay and directed the film. He said he had Johnny in mind for the part from the beginning. "He was the guy I thought about when creating this character," Koepp said. "He's one of our great actors, so inventive and different every time. . . . He is also a completely fearless actor."

In early 2004, forty-year-old Johnny headed for London to begin filming of *The Libertine*. The film told the story of seventeenth-century English poet John Wilmot, the Earl of Rochester. It was a small-budget independent film, far from the big-budget pictures Johnny had favored in recent years. But the character had appealed to him. Rochester was a popular and well-known nobleman, but he refused to obey the rules of polite society. He drank excessively, had public affairs with many women, and made fun of important political figures. The part really allowed Johnny to tap into his own rock-star persona.

"The more I read about Rochester, the more I researched him, I just fell in love with him," Johnny said. "He was an incredibly complicated man and a horribly pained soul."

The film was small and went largely unnoticed by the moviegoing public. *Finding Neverland* had finally been released just two weeks before *The Libertine*'s opening, overshadowing attention it might have

March 8, 2004

Happiness finds Johnny Depp

From the Pages of
USA TODAY

He watches hours of cartoons with his children, has taken up running and is working on his French to better communicate with his companion's parents.

With his fine-boned good looks, longish dark hair and slightly boho [free and unconventional] demeanor, he could still pass for 25, but Johnny Depp is 40. And his days of drugs, drink and trashing hotel rooms are a thing of the past.

Now, he sports three colorful bracelets made by his 5-year-old daughter Lily-Rose. He seems settled, content and, well, grown up.

"I just kind of stumbled around for 35 years," Depp says. "And then when my daughter arrived, it was like 'Now, I see.' Suddenly everything else is just kind of shavings, morsels, little tidbits. And this is what it's all about. This is real life. Boy, it couldn't have come at a better time."

His new movie, *Secret Window*, opens Friday, capping a pretty great time indeed for Depp. He's happily settled down with Vanessa Paradis, a French pop singer, and their children, Lily-Rose and Jack, 23 months. He divides his time between homes in France and Los Angeles. He won a Screen Actors Guild award last month for his staggering, swaggering buccaneer in *Pirates of the Caribbean*. Though he lost the Oscar to Sean Penn, there was a sense that Depp had come awfully close, based on the fact that the onetime bad boy who's still taking chances is now one of Hollywood's most respected actors. His performance as the irresistibly silly swashbuckler Capt. Jack Sparrow was the major reason for the success of Disney's *Pirates of the Caribbean*, which made $305 million.

otherwise gotten. But it was a critical success. Johnny was nominated for a British Independent Film Award.

Earlier in his career, *The Libertine* was exactly the sort of film fans might have expected Johnny to take. But by the mid-2000s, his outlook

Change of scenery: Writer and director David Koepp *(left)* and Depp *(right)* worked together on the film *Secret Window* (2004).

"You put a genius in the middle of a pirate movie and it becomes effervescent," says Gary Ross, who directed another summer hit, *Seabiscuit*. "It would have made $100 million without Johnny Depp."

In *Secret Window*, a psychological thriller based on a Stephen King story, Depp plays a blocked novelist.

"I'd never done a film like this. I read David Koepp's screenplay, and it really kept me on the edge of my seat," he says. "Also, it's nice to go from one extreme like Captain Jack, where the volume's kind of on 11, as it were, then go to something very subdued and internal." For *Secret Window*, Depp insisted on looking disheveled, as a writer deserted by both his wife and his inspiration.

When he spotted a torn, frayed bathrobe in an early costume fitting, "he lunged across the room and said 'This is it,'" Koepp says. "He wanted to wear it for the whole movie."

With the robe, nerdy spectacles and a severe case of bed head, Depp pulls off a witty performance.

"You can rumple him, but you can't make him unattractive," Koepp says. "You can try, but it won't happen."

—Claudia Puig

and approach had changed. He had become one of Hollywood's top leading men, and he had his pick of big-budget films. His fans clamored for more Captain Jack, and it was time for him to give them what they wanted.

Willy Wonka: Depp reunited with director Tim Burton with much box-office success on the 2005 film *Charlie and the Chocolate Factory*.

Hit after Hit

In 2004 Tim Burton asked Johnny to join him for dinner. The director told Johnny that he was working on a film based on the children's story *Charlie and the Chocolate Factory* by Roald Dahl. Burton asked Johnny if he wanted to play the role of Willy Wonka, the mysterious owner of a candy factory. Johnny agreed on the spot. He said he didn't even need to see a script. He knew that if Burton was involved, it would be good.

It would be a challenging role. Millions of people worldwide had read and treasured Dahl's book, first published in 1964. Many more had seen the original film adaptation, 1971's *Willy Wonka and the Chocolate Factory*. That movie is perhaps best remembered for actor Gene Wilder's portrayal of Wonka. To many, the idea of anyone else as Willy Wonka was unthinkable.

Even Wilder questioned the wisdom of a remake. "It's all about money," he said

Iconic Wonka: Depp had big shoes to fill when taking on the role of Willa Wonka. Actor Gene Wilder *(above)* played the character in the 1971 movie adaptation of the book by Roald Dahl.

in an interview. "Why else would you remake *Willy Wonka*? I don't see the point in going back and doing it all over again. I like Johnny Depp, and I appreciate that he has said on record that my shoes will be hard to fill. But I don't know how it will turn out."

Wilder was far from alone in questioning the wisdom of remaking what many felt was a classic film. But Burton and Johnny had their own ideas. They set out to make the 2005 version of the eccentric Willy Wonka noticeably different from Wilder's iconic 1971 version. While Wilder's version of the character is cheerful yet stern, Johnny's version is strange, dark, and more than a little creepy.

Tim Burton

It's no secret who Johnny's favorite director and closest Hollywood friend is. It's Tim Burton. The pair have worked together on seven films—with more almost certainly to come.

Burton was born in Burbank, California, on August 25, 1958. From a young age, he was fascinated by film. He loved monster movies and even shot his own short films with a small camera. He attended the California Institute of the Arts before being hired as an artist at Walt Disney Productions in 1979. Burton's big break as a filmmaker came with 1985's *Pee-Wee's Big Adventure*. The film focused on the TV character Pee Wee Herman (Paul Reubens). Three years later, Burton's *Beetlejuice* was released, and he was officially a big-time Hollywood director.

Burton's star rose with 1989's *Batman* and 1990's *Edward Scissorhands*, the film that began his longtime friendship and collaboration with Johnny. Burton had gained a reputation for making dark and quirky films. He was different, and he was in demand. His other films include 1993's animated *The Night-*

Fruitful friendship: Burton *(back)* and Depp *(front)* became close friends while working together on seven movies.

mare Before Christmas (which he wrote and produced but did not direct), 2001's *Planet of the Apes*, and 2003's *Big Fish*.

The film's familiar story, along with the Burton-Depp artistic touch, made it a box-office success. The critics gave mixed reviews. Some praised Johnny's courage in the role and Burton's faithfulness to Dahl's book. Others found Johnny's performance overdone. "The cumulative effect isn't pretty," wrote Ann Hornaday of the *Washington Post.* "Nor is it kooky, funny, eccentric, or even mildly interesting. Indeed, throughout his fey, simpering performance, Depp seems to be straining so hard for weirdness that the entire enterprise begins to feel like those excruciating occasions when your parents tried to be hip. If you have to try that hard, you just aren't."

A Return to the High Seas

While still working on *Charlie and the Chocolate Factory*, Burton and Depp began another project. Burton was making an animated film titled *Corpse Bride*, about a young man who accidentally marries a dead woman. Johnny provided the voice of the young man, Victor. However, Johnny hadn't realized that his work on *Corpse Bride* would overlap with the filming of *Charlie*. This left him little time to prepare for his role as Victor.

Voice work: In Burton's animated film *Corpse Bride* (2005), Depp voiced the main character, Victor Van Dort *(left)*. Burton's companion, actress Helena Bonham Carter, did the voice work for the title character *(right)*.

Johnny regretted what he saw as his carelessness. "I should be flogged," he said at the time. "It somehow didn't occur to me that we were going to be doing it at the same time [as *Charlie*]. I thought it was going to be like months down the road so I would have some time to prepare for the character. So you could imagine my surprise when, as I was very, very focused on Wonka, Tim [Burton] arrives on set and says 'Hey, you know maybe tonight we'll go and record some of *Corpse Bride*.' I was like, sure, of course we can. I have no character. I didn't know what the guy was going to sound like or anything."

Despite Johnny's concerns about his lack of preparation, *Corpse Bride* was a success. Next, forty-three-year-old Johnny returned to the role of Captain Jack. He had agreed to two more *Pirates of the Caribbean* films. The two movies, subtitled *Dead Man's Chest* and *At World's End*, would be filmed back-to-back. *Dead Man's Chest* would be released in summer 2006 and *At World's End* in summer 2007.

Jack is back: Depp *(far right)* donned Captain Jack Sparrow's duds again for two *Pirates of the Caribbean* sequels. Here he acts out a scene from *Dead Man's Chest* (2006) in front of the cameras with co-stars Orlando Bloom *(center)* and Keira Knightley *(second from right)*.

"I went through a decompression period after the first film," Johnny said. "If you're really connected with a character, you always do to some degree. You miss the guy. You miss being that person. The only thing that was in the back of my mind was the hope that there would be a sequel someday, so that I could meet him again."

Johnny signed a $60 million contract for the two sequels. That amount of money might have seemed excessive to some in the movie business. But Disney executives fully understood that the sequels

IN FOCUS

The HMS *Bounty*

For *Dead Man's Chest*, Johnny and his fellow actors got to board a ship called the HMS *Bounty*. This ship was originally built in 1960 for the film *Mutiny on the Bounty* (which starred Johnny's friend Marlon Brando). It was the first full-scale, operational ship ever built just for a movie. The ship was built to look like the original *Bounty*, a British ship of the late 1700s. The *Bounty* was most famous for a mutiny (overthrow of the captain) that took place in 1789. In *Dead Man's Chest*, the ship went by the name *Edinburgh Trader*.

Faithful ship: The cast of the second *Pirates of the Caribbean* movie used the famous film ship the HMS *Bounty* as part of the set.

July 10, 2006

'Pirates' captures biggest opening ever

<u>From the Pages of</u>
<u>USA TODAY</u>

Pirates of the Caribbean: Dead Man's Chest surpassed virtually every box-office debut achievement on record this weekend, capturing the biggest opening in movie history.

The Johnny Depp adventure took in a staggering $132 million in its first three days, according to studio estimates from box-office trackers Nielsen EDI.

The debut easily shatters the record held by 2002's *Spider-Man*, which opened to $114.8 million.

The milestones didn't stop there. The sequel to the 2003 smash became the first film to rake in $100 million in two days. It did $55.5 million on Friday, the biggest single-day haul for any movie, eclipsing *Star Wars* Episode III*: Revenge of the Sith*, which did $50 million in one day last year.

"They're mind-blowing numbers," says Chuck Viane, distribution chief for Disney, which released *Pirates*. "We knew it would be a big movie, but I don't think would be big moneymakers. And they knew that without Johnny Depp, the movies would never happen. Studio executives reportedly gave the scriptwriters some guidelines for what they wanted: Jack Sparrow, Jack Sparrow, and more Jack Sparrow.

Although the films continued the story from the first Pirates movie, each also stood on its own. Both followed the exploits of Sparrow, Will Turner (played by Orlando Bloom), and Elizabeth Swann (Keira Knightley). Johnny knew that moviegoers would expect lots of action, great special effects, and plenty of humor. In those regards, the movies did not disappoint.

anyone knew it was going to be part of a pirate-chic phenomenon. That's what really helped make it huge."

The film arrived riding a crest of pirate mania. Retailers are selling everything from T-shirts to dinner plates emblazoned with skulls and crossbones. Disneyland's theme park ride reopened Monday with 4,500 people waiting 3½ hours in line to see the new versions of Depp's Captain Jack Sparrow and Geoffrey Rush's pirate Barbossa.

"It's still a relatively new film franchise, but Jack Sparrow is already an icon for a young generation," says Chad Hartigan, a box-office analyst for Reelsource. "He has an appeal we haven't seen in the movies for some time."

Depp initially mortified Disney executives with his decision to play Sparrow as a loopy, smirking and sometimes effeminate pirate.

But after the first film sailed to $305 million, those executives asked him to ham it up even more for this movie and the third installment, *Pirates of the Caribbean: At World's End*, due May 25.

"You have to give all the credit in the world to Johnny," Viane says. "He's created a character people want to dress like, be like. They can't get enough of him."

Even competing studios had to tip their hats to the film, which helped drive ticket sales for the top 12 movies 50 percent over the same weekend last year.

"Kudos to Disney," says Rory Bruer, distribution chief for Sony Pictures, which released *Spider-Man*. "This is the kind of thing that gets people excited about going to the movies."

—Scott Bowles

Still, Johnny and director Gore Verbinski pushed the limits when they could. Disney executives no longer had reservations about the way Johnny was portraying Sparrow, but Johnny admitted to going out of his way to give the character new and greater levels of weirdness. And Verbinski even brought in Keith Richards—one of Johnny's models for Sparrow—for a role in the film.

"It's a sort of gambit," Verbinski said, explaining the risks he and Depp took. "We're both really uncomfortable if other people are comfortable. You worry, 'Are we phoning it in?' If executives are going to sleep well at night, well, you don't want that."

To no one's surprise, the strategy worked. *Dead Man's Chest* took in a record $55 million on its first day alone and went on to gross more than $1 billion worldwide. It also earned Johnny another Golden Globe nomination for Best Actor.

The third film, *At World's End*, fell into the same mold, though many criticized the plot as being unnecessarily complicated and wandering. Captain Jack Sparrow was at his flamboyant best, however, so most audiences didn't mind. The film had the highest budget of the three—and the highest of all time for any film—at $300 million. But with a worldwide gross of $960 million, *At World's End* turned an easy profit. Johnny won an MTV Movie Award and a Teen Choice Award for his performance.

Singing Barber

Johnny was more popular than ever, and he had Captain Jack Sparrow to thank for it. But that didn't mean he was leaving behind other roles. After filming on *At World's End* wrapped up, Johnny focused on his next project, *Sweeney Todd: The Demon Barber of Fleet Street*. The film once again reunited him with Tim Burton.

Sweeney Todd is a musical—an unusual choice for both Burton and Johnny. The screenplay was adapted from a popular Broadway musical about Benjamin Barker, a fictional barber in nineteenth-century London. Barker is wrongly convicted of a crime by a corrupt judge. After fifteen years in prison, Barker takes the name Sweeney Todd and returns to London to get his revenge.

Johnny had a musical background but had little vocal training. When Burton first offered him the role, Johnny had been unsure whether to accept. He recalled telling Burton, "I'm going to go into the studio with a pal of mine and I'm going to investigate and try and sing the songs, and if I'm close, then we can talk about it, or I'll call you and say, 'You know what, I can't do it. It's just impossible.'"

The trial run must have gone well, because Johnny decided to take the risk—with the help of some vocal coaching. Filming began in

Hitting a high note: Depp tried something new with his role in *Sweeney Todd: The Demon Barber of Fleet Street* (2007). He had to sing throughout the movie.

February 2007. But a month into filming, Johnny had to rush home. Lily-Rose had become seriously ill from food poisoning. Johnny and Paradis stayed by her side at the hospital for nine days, at times fearing for her life. He later called it the scariest thing he'd ever experienced. When Johnny was sure that Lily-Rose was safe, he returned to filming.

The film's sound track (album of songs) was released on December 18, 2007—three days before the film itself. Critics said that Johnny didn't have the best voice, but that he sang forcefully and with conviction. Considering his lack of vocal experience, that may have been the best review he could have hoped for.

The film grossed $9 million in its opening weekend and went on to gross more than $150 million worldwide. That was an impressive figure for a musical, a format that often does poorly at the box office.

The movie was an even bigger hit with critics. "Johnny Depp is ideally cast," wrote *USA Today*'s Claudia Puig. "He's undeniably one of the best actors of his generation, and there are hints of his past collaborations with Burton in his performance. You'll catch glimpses of Edward Scissorhands, Ed Wood and Victor from *Corpse Bride*."

Johnny's powerful performance earned him an Academy Award nomination for Best Actor. He lost to Daniel Day-Lewis from *There Will Be Blood*. But he won the Golden Globe and the film won the Golden Globe in the category of Best Motion Picture—Comedy or Musical.

Hero and Villain

In early 2008, director Terry Gilliam (who had worked with Johnny on *Fear and Loathing in Las Vegas*) was filming a new project, *The Imaginarium of Doctor Parnassus*. The film starred twenty-eight-year-old Heath Ledger, an up-and-coming actor and a friend of Johnny's. But on January 22, with filming about half done, tragedy struck. Ledger died suddenly from a drug overdose. Filming was suspended, and Hollywood mourned the loss of one of its stars.

Gilliam was in a difficult position. Should he stop filming and cancel the project? Or should he press on? He decided to continue with the project. Gilliam chose to use three actors—Johnny, Colin Farrell, and Jude Law—to take on Ledger's role of Tony in the film. All three actors agreed to donate their salaries to Ledger's young daughter.

Johnny was in the middle of filming another movie, *Public Enemies*. So he had to shoot all of his *Imaginarium* scenes in just a day and a half. He later said, "Though the circumstances of my involvement are extremely heart-rending and unbelievably sad, I feel privileged to have been asked aboard to stand in on behalf of dear Heath."

Johnny then returned to filming *Public Enemies*, which tells the tale of 1930s American gangster John Dillinger and his associates. Depp plays Dillinger, a bank robber who many people saw, at the time, as something of a modern-day Robin Hood.

Playing the enemy: Depp wore 1930s period clothes to play real-life gangster John Dillinger in Michael Mann's film *Public Enemies* (2009).

"Especially in that era . . . everything was going against the common man," Johnny said of Dillinger's appeal. "People like John Dillinger came back and were anti the establishment in their own special way. I actually hope people root for him."

Some critics said the movie had failed to realize its full potential and painted too narrow a picture of Dillinger and of the period. But the film was generally well received by fans and critics. *USA Today*'s Claudia Puig wrote, "An action film that feels like an epic, *Public Enemies* is an exciting and stylish slice of Americana." The film didn't receive a single Academy Award or Golden Globe nomination. Yet it grossed more than $200 million, proving once again that Johnny was box-office gold.

CHAPTER EIGHT

Honored by the people: Depp accepts a People's Choice Award for Favorite Movie Actor in January 2010.

Modern-Day Rebel

■■■■■

Johnny's life and career have changed a great deal since he took his first acting job in 1984. At first, he didn't even want to be an actor. Later, he embraced his career but shied away from the spotlight, preferring character roles and often going out of his way to avoid being labeled as just another leading man. But in recent years, Johnny's choices have changed. While he still is on the lookout for interesting, compelling, and sometimes off-beat characters, he seems to have found peace with the idea of being a major Hollywood star.

In January 2010, he was on hand at the People's Choice Awards in Los Angeles. He was honored as Favorite Movie Actor and Favorite Movie Actor of the Decade. Johnny, never comfortable with public praise, graciously accepted the awards.

"I'm deeply humbled by this great honor," Johnny told the crowd. "This comes from you, the people, which means everything to me, certainly. It means everything to us all because the only reason any of us are up here is because of you, so thank you for that. It has been an amazing decade."

The Mad Hatter

While filming *Public Enemies*, Johnny had received a call from his old friend Tim Burton. The director was working on a film based on author Lewis Carroll's famous stories *Alice's Adventures in Wonderland* and *Through the Looking Glass*. In Carroll's books, Alice is an English girl

Depp in wonderland: Depp teamed up with Burton again for the 2010 film *Alice in Wonderland*.

IN F⊕CUS

Character Actor

The role of the Mad Hatter promised to be challenging for any actor. But Johnny, with his love of oddball characters, was well suited to it. He knew that no matter how strange—or mad—the character, the key to success is finding a connection to the role. Tim Burton explained the actor's approach. "[Johnny] tried to find a grounding to the character [the Mad Hatter]," Burton said, "something that you feel, as opposed to just being mad. In a lot of versions it's a very one-note kind of character and you know his goal was to try and bring out a human side to the strangeness of the character. Any time I work with him that's something he tries to do so that's no exception."

Mad Hatter: To play the Mad Hatter, Depp wore makeup that made him almost unrecognizable.

who finds herself lost in a dreamlike world full of strange creatures. One of the most memorable characters she meets is the Mad Hatter. Burton's film would tell the tale of Alice's return to Wonderland as a young woman. Burton wanted Depp to be his Mad Hatter. Even though Carroll had created the character almost 150 years before, it seemed like a part written for Johnny.

Johnny was interested, having just reread the original *Adventures in Wonderland*. So once again, he agreed to work with his friend—the seventh time the pair had collaborated on a movie.

"[Burton] couldn't have bitten off anything bigger to chew," Johnny said. "This is almost lunatic time. To choose to grab *Alice in Wonderland*, that in itself is one thing, and then to do it to the Tim Burton level is madness. . . . It's the greatest undertaking I've heard of."

IN FOCUS

In Focus: The Green Screen

Most of *Alice in Wonderland* was shot in front of a green screen. The green screen has long been used for films featuring a lot of special effects or artificial backgrounds. Everything except the actors and their props shows up green on the film. Computers later replace the green with digital content. For example, a green background can be turned into a fantastic forest.

The advantage of using green-screen technology is obvious. It allows directors to take audiences to places that don't exist in the real world. But that doesn't mean the technology comes without costs.

Actors have to place themselves in a scene that's not really there. They have to pretend to see and react to things that aren't there. It makes the acting process much more labor-intensive and less natural.

"The novelty of the green wears off very quickly," Johnny said in an interview during filming of *Alice in Wonderland*. "It's exhausting, actually. I mean, I like an obstacle. I don't mind having to spew dialogue while...some guy is holding a card and I'm talking to a piece of tape. But the green beats you up. You're kind of befuddled at the end of the day."

June 22, 2009

What a weird 'Wonderland' Burton made

From the Pages of
USA TODAY

You might have gone down the rabbit hole before. But never with a guide quite as attuned to the fantastic as Tim Burton.

Those who have grown curiouser and curiouser about what the offbeat reinventor of *Charlie and the Chocolate Factory* might conjure up in his version of *Alice in Wonderland* can feast their eyes on this array of concept art and publicity images, due to hang in movie theaters this week.

"It has been Burton-ized" is how producer Richard Zanuck describes the director's vision of the Lewis Carroll classic. Many elements are familiar, from the enigmatic Caterpillar (Alan Rickman) to the fierce Jabberwock (Christopher Lee). But none has been presented in this sort of visually surreal fashion.

"We finished shooting in December after only 40 days," Zanuck says. Now the live action is being merged with CG (computer) animation and motion-capture creatures, and then transferred into 3-D. The traditional tale has been freshened with a blast of girl power, courtesy of writer Linda Woolverton (*Beauty and the Beast*). Alice, 17, attends a party at a Victorian estate only to find she is about to be proposed to in front of hundreds of snooty society types. Off she runs, following a white rabbit into a hole and ending up in Wonderland, a place she visited 10 years before yet doesn't remember.

Among those who welcome her back is the Mad Hatter, a part tailor-made for Johnny Depp as he collaborates with Burton for the seventh time. "This character is off his rocker," Zanuck says.

Aussie (Australian) actress Mia Wasikowska, 19, best known for HBO's *In Treatment*, has the coveted title role. "There is something real, honest and sincere about her," Zanuck says. "She's not a typical Hollywood starlet."

There is the usual Burton-esque ghoulishness (Helena Bonham Carter's Red Queen, whose favorite retort is "Off with their heads," has a moat (pond) filled with bobbing noggins (floating heads), but Zanuck assures most kids can handle it. "The book itself is pretty dark," he notes. "This is for little people and people who read it when they were little 50 years ago."

—Susan Wloszczyna

Alice in Wonderland opened March 5, 2010, to massive crowds. It grossed $116 million in its opening weekend, shattering the record for a film opening in March. Within a month, it had grossed close to $800 million worldwide. While critical response to the film was mixed, moviegoers were eager to see Burton's vision of the classic story.

Johnny's Future

Johnny's career has taken off, but he continues to focus on his family. He enjoys spending time with his two children. Rumors about Johnny and Paradis getting married have swirled for years. In 2007 reports said that Lily-Rose's serious illness caused the couple to decide to tie the knot. In 2008 reports said that Johnny was shopping for engagement rings. Reports surfaced again early in 2010 (some even named

So happy together: Paradis and Depp attend the Cannes Film Festival in France in May 2010.

Tim Burton as his best man), but still the couple remains happy with their living arrangement. Considering Johnny's experiences with marriages and engagements early in his life, it's not hard to understand why he might not want to mess with a good thing.

"Each summer people say we're supposed to be getting married," Paradis said in late 2008. "But we don't talk about it that much. He's got me, and he knows he's got me. . . . I love the romance of 'let's get married,' but then, when you have it so perfect . . . I mean, I'm more married than anybody can be. We have two kids. Maybe one day, but it's something I can really do without."

Professionally, Johnny has a lot of plans for the near future. Fans of Captain Jack Sparrow were excited when he had signed on to do a fourth *Pirates of the Caribbean* movie, to be subtitled *On Stranger Tides*. The movie, which will not include Knightley and Bloom, is scheduled to be filmed in the summer of 2010 and released in 2011. The story will reportedly center on the search for the mythical Fountain of Youth.

Other films on the horizon include *The Rum Diary*, which completed filming in early 2010. The film is based on a novel by Hunter

On location: Depp waves to the cameras from the set of *The Rum Diary* in San Juan, Puerto Rico, in 2009.

Famous costars: Depp *(right)* and costar Angelina Jolie *(front left)* filmed *The Tourist* on location in Venice, Italy, in 2010.

S. Thompson, Johnny's friend and the author of *Fear and Loathing in Las Vegas*. The film *The Tourist*, an action-thriller, will feature Johnny as an American tourist in Italy who becomes unwittingly embroiled in a criminal drama. Johnny has been rumored to be tied to many other films, ranging from a remake of *Dark Shadows* (a supernatural TV soap opera from the late 1960s and early 1970s) to *Dalí* (a biopic about Spanish artist Salvador Dalí).

As Johnny has proved time and again, however, predicting the types of roles he will accept is all but impossible. His place among Hollywood actors is unique. So many leading men are obsessed with stardom. But while Johnny has come to terms with his fame, he never wanted it. His choices of roles have, for more than two decades, been the source of—at times—criticism, disbelief, and admiration. His brave and sometimes seemingly reckless role choices, as well as his behavior off the set, have truly earned him the title Hollywood Rebel.

TIMELINE

1963   Johnny Depp is born in Owensboro, Kentucky.

1978   Johnny's parents divorce. Johnny chooses to live in Florida with his mother.

1980   Johnny forms a band, the Kids.

1983   Johnny marries Lori Anne Allison. Johnny, Allison, and the Kids move to Los Angeles.

1984   Johnny stars in his first movie, *A Nightmare on Elm Street*.

1985   Johnny is cast in a major Hollywood project, *Platoon*. He spends months in the Philippines filming the war drama.

1987   *Platoon* premieres to critical acclaim, but in the final cut, Johnny's role is trimmed to just a few lines. Johnny reluctantly agrees to star as a young undercover cop in the TV series *21 Jump Street*.

1989   Johnny attempts to limit typecasting by signing up for *Cry-Baby*, a musical comedy film. He begins dating fellow actor Winona Ryder.

1990   Johnny leaves *21 Jump Street*. He and Ryder star in director Tim Burton's movie *Edward Scissorhands*. The couple's on-and-off relationship becomes a media sensation.

1993   Johnny stars in three films, *Arizona Dream*, *Benny & Joon*, and *What's Eating Gilbert Grape*. He buys a partial interest in the Viper Room, a West Hollywood nightclub. Johnny comes under criticism when young actor River Phoenix dies at the club.

1994   After a fight with supermodel girlfriend Kate Moss, Johnny is arrested at a New York City hotel. Johnny joins Tim Burton again for the biopic *Ed Wood*.

1995   Johnny's career flags with the critical and commercial failures of *Don Juan DeMarco*, *Dead Man*, and *Nick of Time*.

1997   Johnny wins critical acclaim for his role as an FBI agent in *Donnie Brasco*. He signs on to play writer Hunter S. Thompson in *Fear and Loathing in Las Vegas*.

1998   While filming *The Ninth Gate* in Paris, Johnny meets French performer Vanessa Paradis. The two begin living together.

1999   Johnny and Paradis's daughter, Lily-Rose, is born. The couple decides to live fulltime in France. *Sleepy Hollow*, starring Johnny as Ichabod Crane, earns more than $100 million at the box office.

2000   Johnny plays a gay Cuban man in *Before Night Falls* and a free-spirited visitor to a French village in *Chocolat*.

2001   Johnny is given a star on the Hollywood Walk of Fame. He creates a media firestorm after condemning life in the United States and its political leadership. His films *Blow* and *From Hell* are released to moderate success.

2002   Johnny and Paradis's son, Jack, is born.

2003   Johnny creates the unique character Captain Jack Sparrow for the summer blockbuster *Pirates of the Caribbean: The Curse of the Black Pearl*. He again draws media attention for criticizing the United States.

2004   Johnny's movies *Secret Window* and *Finding Neverland* are released. He begins filming the historical drama *The Libertine* in London, England.

2005   Johnny and Tim Burton team up for two films—*Charlie and the Chocolate Factory* and *Corpse Bride*.

2006   Johnny returns to the role of Jack Sparrow in *Pirates of the Caribbean: Dead Man's Chest*.

2007   The third *Pirates of the Caribbean* installment, *At World's End*, is released. Johnny earns an Academy Award nomination for *Sweeney Todd: The Demon Barber of Fleet Street*.

2008   Johnny joins the cast of *The Imaginarium of Doctor Parnassus* to help fill the lead role after the death of actor Heath Ledger.

2009   Johnny plays legendary gangster John Dillinger in *Public Enemies*.

2010   In his seventh film with Tim Burton, Johnny takes on the role of the Mad Hatter in *Alice in Wonderland*.

GLOSSARY

audition: a trial performance. In an audition, an actor tries out for a part by reading a bit of script for the director or producers.

biopic: a biographical film about a real person's life

blockbuster: a large, expensive movie, usually very popular with the general public

cameo: a brief and often uncredited appearance by a star or celebrity in a film or television show

green screen: a technique for filming special effects scenes. The actors play their parts in front of a big green screen (or sometimes a blue screen). Computers later exchange the green in the picture with special effects.

gross: a money total figured before costs are deducted. A movie's gross is the money made at movie theaters from ticket sales, without subtracting actor's salaries, production expenses, and other costs.

Mafia: a large organized crime group that originated on the Italian island of Sicily

paparazzi: photographers who make a living by taking unauthorized photos of celebrities and selling the photos to publications

pilot: the first episode of a new television show

producer: a person who oversees the planning and financing of a television show, film, record, or other form of entertainment

punk rock: a form of rock and roll characterized by a fast tempo, loudness, and aggressive lyrics that often express alienation from society

screenplay: the script and filming directions for a movie or a television show

sound track: a collection of music used in a film

typecast: to always cast an actor in the same type of role

FILMOGRAPHY

A Nightmare on Elm Street
Role: Glen Lantz
Released: 1984
Director: Wes Craven

Private Resort
Role: Jack Marshall
Released: 1985
Director: George Bowers

Slow Burn
Role: Donnie Fleischer
Released: 1986
Director: Matthew Chapman

Platoon
Role: Private Gator Lerner
Released: 1986
Director: Oliver Stone

Cry-Baby
Role: Wade "Cry-Baby" Walker
Released: 1990
Director: John Waters

Edward Scissorhands
Role: Edward Scissorhands
Released: 1990
Director: Tim Burton

Benny & Joon
Role: Sam
Released: 1993
Director: Jeremiah S. Chechik

Arizona Dream
Role: Axel Blackmar
Released: 1993
Director: Emir Kusturica

What's Eating Gilbert Grape
Role: Gilbert Grape
Released: 1993
Director: Lasse Hallström

Ed Wood
Role: Ed Wood
Released: 1994
Director: Tim Burton

Don Juan DeMarco
Role: Don Juan
Released: 1995
Director: Jeremy Leven

Dead Man
Role: William Blake
Released: 1995
Director: Jim Jarmusch

Nick of Time
Role: Gene Watson
Released: 1995
Director: John Badham

Donnie Brasco
Role: Joe Pistone/Donnie Brasco
Released : 1997
Director: Mike Newell

The Brave
Role: Raphael
Released: 1997
Director: Johnny Depp

Fear and Loathing in Las Vegas
Role: Raoul Duke
Released: 1998
Director: Terry Gilliam

The Ninth Gate
Role: Dean Corso
Released: 1999
Director: Roman Polanski

The Astronaut's Wife
Role: Spencer Armacost
Released: 1999
Director: Rand Ravich

Sleepy Hollow
Role: Ichabod Crane
Released: 1999
Director: Tim Burton

The Man Who Cried
Role: Cesar
Released: 2000
Director: Sally Potter

Before Night Falls
Roles: Bon Bon/Lieutenant Victor
Released: 2000
Director: Julian Schnabel

Chocolat
Role: Roux
Released: 2000
Director: Lasse Hallström

Blow
Role: George Jung
Released: 2001
Director: Ted Demme

From Hell
Role: Frederick Abberline
Released: 2001
Directors: Albert Hughes and Allen Hughes

Pirates of the Caribbean: The Curse of the Black Pearl
Role: Jack Sparrow
Released: 2003
Director: Gore Verbinski

Once Upon a Time in Mexico
Role: Sheldon Sands
Released: 2003
Director: Robert Rodriguez

Secret Window
Role: Mort Rainey
Released: 2004
Director: David Koepp

Finding Neverland
Role: J. M. Barrie
Released: 2004
Director: Marc Forster

The Libertine
Role: Rochester
Released: 2004
Director: Laurence Dunmore

Charlie and the Chocolate Factory
Role: Willy Wonka
Released: 2005
Director: Tim Burton

Corpse Bride
Role: Victor Van Dort (voice)
Released: 2005
Directors: Tim Burton and Mike
Johnson

**Pirates of the Caribbean: Dead
Man's Chest**
Role: Jack Sparrow
Released: 2006
Director: Gore Verbinski

**Pirates of the Caribbean: At
World's End**
Role: Jack Sparrow
Released: 2007
Director: Gore Verbinski

**Sweeney Todd: The Demon Barber
of Fleet Street**
Role: Sweeney Todd/Benjamin
Barker
Released: 2007
Director: Tim Burton

**The Imaginarium of Doctor
Parnassus**
Role: Imaginarium Tony #1
Released: 2009
Director: Terry Gilliam

Public Enemies
Role: John Dillinger
Released: 2009
Director: Michael Mann

Alice in Wonderland
Role: Mad Hatter
Released: 2010
Director: Tim Burton

SOURCE NOTES

5   Nigen Goodall, *The Secret World of Johnny Depp* (London: Blake, 2007), 52.

7   Denis Meikle, *Johnny Depp: A Kind of Illusion* (London: Reynolds & Hearn, 2006), 69.

9   Ibid., 23.

9   Ibid., 22.

11   Michael Blitz and Louise Krasniewicz, *Johnny Depp: A Biography* (Westport, CT: Greenwood Press, 2008), 11.

11   Martyn Palmer, "Johnny's Treasure Chest," *Mail on Sunday*, May 20, 2007, http://interview.johnnydepp-zone2.com/2007_0520TheMailOnSunday.html (August 23, 2010).

12   Tom Green, "Johnny Depp Cuts Free;'Jump Street' Cuteness Still Dogs Him," *USA Today*, April 3, 1990.

13   Meikle, 36.

14   Ibid, 40.

15   Ibid, 45.

17   Goodall, 43.

21   Meikle, 75.

22   Tom Green, "Where to Find Mr. Cool? Address: '21 Jump Street'," *USA Today*, January 28, 1988.

23   Goodall, 56.

27   Ibid., 69.

29   Ibid., 92.

32   Meikle, 97.

32   Goodall, 117.

34   Roger Ebert, review of *What's Eating Gilbert Grape*, directed by Lasse Hallström, *Chicago Sun-Times*, March 4, 1994, http://rogerebert.suntimes.com/apps/pbcs.dll/article?AID=/19940304/REVIEWS/403040305/1023 (August 23, 2010).

35   Goodall, 135.

35   Dan Yakir, "Truly Madly Deeply," *Sky*, April 1994.

40   Goodall, 181–182.

45   Jessamy Calkin, "Johnny Depp, Esq.," *Esquire* (UK edition), February 2000.

46   Ibid.

47–48   Goodall, 223.

48–49   Ibid., 223.

49   Susan Wloszczyna, "'Donnie Brasco.' A High Point for Lowlifes," *USA Today*, February 28, 1997.

50   Janet Maslin, review of *Donnie Brasco*, directed by Mike Newell, *New York Times*, February 28, 1997.

50   Goodall, 238.

51   Ibid., 240.

58   Meikle, 256–257.

60   Goodall, 266.

62   Meikle, 266.

63   Goodall, 273.

63   Mike Clark, "Depp Delivers as Shady Character 'Blow' Uses Cocaine Story, Novel Casting to Full Advantage," *USA Today*, April 6, 2001.

69   Goodall, 316–317.

69–70   Meikle, 324.

70   Anthony Breznican, "Johnny Depp Plays It His Way; This 'Pirate' of an Actor Is Still Going Strong-Minded," *USA Today*, June 26, 2006.

71   Goodall, 347.

73   Claudia Puig, "Yo-Ho-Ho and a Bottle of . . . Fun!; 'Pirates' Has It All: Thrills, Humor, Cool Characters," *USA Today*, July 9, 2003.

73   Roger Ebert, review of *Pirates of the Caribbean: The Curse of the Black Pearl*, directed by Gore Verbinski, *Chicago Sun-Times*, July 9, 2003, http://rogerebert.suntimes.com/apps/pbcs.dll/article?AID=/20030709/REVIEWS/307090301/1023 (August 23, 2010).

73   Goodall, 290.

74   Claudia Puig, "Depp Fans Flames in Quirky 'Mexico," *USA Today*, September 12, 2003.

74   Stephan M. Silverman, "Johnny Depp Calls U.S. a 'Dumb Puppy,'" *People*, September 4, 2003, http://www.people.com/people/article/0,,626682,00.html (September 3, 2010).

75   Goodall, 295.

75   Ibid., 305.

79   Meikle, 359.

81   Ann Hornaday, "Sorry, Charlie," *Washington Post*, July 15, 2005, http://www.washingtonpost.com/wp-dyn/content/article/2005/07/14/AR2005071402083.html (August 23, 2010).

106 USA TODAY · **Johnny Depp:** Hollywood Rebel

82 Goodall, 336.

83 Meilke, 367.

85 Anthony Breznican, "Johnny Depp Plays It His Way; This 'Pirate' of an Actor Is Still Going Strong-Minded," *USA Today*, June 26, 2006.

86 Emanuel Levy, "Sweeney Todd: The Making of a Musical Movie," emanuellevy.com, n.d., http://www.emanuellevy.com/search/details .cfm?id=8130 (August 23, 2010).

88 Claudia Puig, "'Sweeney Todd': A Sharp Adaptation with a Comedic Edge," *USA Today*, December 21, 2007.

88 Gregory Ellwood, "Johnny Depp Finally Discusses Stepping in for Heath Ledger in 'Imaginarium'," Hitfix.com, December 28, 2009, http:// www.hitfix.com/articles/2009-12-28-johnny-depp-finally-discusses-stepping-in-for-heath-ledger-in-imaginarium (August 23, 2010).

89 Kelley L. Carter, "'Public Enemies' Star Johnny Depp Enjoys Comparisons to the Other J.D.," *USA Today*, June 24, 2009, http://www.usatoday.com/life/people/2009-06-24-publicenemies_N.htm (August 23, 2010).

89 Claudia Puig, "'Public Enemies': Dillinger Captured at Last," *USA Today*, July 1, 2009.

91 *Post Chronicle*, "Sandra Bullock Wins Big at People's Choice Awards," January 7, 2010, http://www.postchronicle.com/cgi-bin/artman/exec/ view.cgi?archive=178&num=277413 (September 3, 2010).

92 Kellen Rice, "Comic-Con 2009: Tim Burton Talks Wonderland," *Blast*, July 23, 2009, http://blastmagazine.com/the-magazine/ entertainment/2009/07/tim-burton-talks-wonderland (August 23, 2010).

93 Mark Salisbury, "Tim Burton and Johnny Depp interview for Alice in Wonderland," *Telegraph*, February 15, 2010, http://www.telegraph. co.uk/culture/film/starsandstories/7205720/Tim-Burton-and-Johnny-Depp-interview-for-Alice-In-Wonderland.html (September 3, 2010).

93 Ibid.

96 Courtney Rubin, "Vanessa Paradis Opens Up About Her Romance with Johnny Depp," *People*, October 13, 2008, http://www.people.com/ people/article/0,,20232623,00.html (August 23, 2010).

SELECTED BIBLIOGRAPHY

Blitz, Michael, and Louise Krasniewicz. *Johnny Depp: A Biography*. Westport, CT: Greenwood Press, 2008.

Goodall, Nigel. *The Secret World of Johnny Depp: An Intimate Biography of Hollywood's Best-Loved Rebel*. London: Blake Publishing, 2007.

Heard, Christopher. *Depp*. Toronto: ECW Press, 2001.

Meikle, Denis. *Johnny Depp: A Kind of Illusion*. London: Reynolds & Hearn, 2006.

FURTHER READING AND WEBSITES

Books

Casey, Jo, and Laura Gilbert. *Alice in Wonderland: The Visual Guide*. New York: DK, 2010.

Graziano, Jim. *Johnny Depp*. Philadelphia: Mason Crest Publishers, 2008.

Higgins, Kara. *Johnny Depp*. San Diego: Lucent Books, 2004.

Kushner, Jill Menkes. *Johnny Depp: Movie Megastar*. Berkeley Heights, NJ: Enslow Publishers, 2010.

Lynette, Rachel. *Tim Burton, Filmmaker*. San Diego: KidHaven Press, 2006.

Steele, Philip. *World of Pirates*. Boston: Kingfisher, 2004.

Wessling, Katherine. *Backstage at a Movie Set*. New York: Children's Press, 2003.

Wine, Bill. *Johnny Depp*. Philadelphia: Mason Crest Publishers, 2009.

Websites

Internet Movie Database
  http://www.imdb.com
  This online resource allows you to look up movies, actors, plot summaries, and more. The site includes a biography of Johnny Depp as well as a list of his projects.

Johnny Depp Fan Page
  http://www.johnnydeppfan.com
  This page, operated by Johnny Depp fans, includes the latest updates on Johnny's films and other projects, as well as photos, a filmography, and much more.

People Magazine—Johnny Depp
  http://www.people.com/people/johnny_depp
  People's page devoted to Johnny Depp includes fun facts, a biography, a timeline, photos, and more.

USA Today
  http://www.usatoday.com
  The home page of *USA Today* provides the latest news, including what's happening in entertainment.

INDEX

PHOTO ACKNOWLEDGMENTS

The images in this book are used with the permission of: REUTERS/Mario Anzuoni, p. 1; © Armando Gallo/Retna Ltd., pp. 3, 91; 20th Century Fox Television/The Kobal Collection, p. 4; © Stephen J. Cannell Productions/Courtesy: Everett Collection, p. 5; © Jim Smeal/ WireImage/Getty Images, pp. 6, 22; © Wikimedia Foundation , Inc./Smallbones, p. 8; BEImages/Rex Features USA, p. 9; Seth Poppel Yearbook Library, p. 10; Rex Features USA, pp. 12, 49; © Barry King/WireImage/Getty Images, p. 14; © New Line Cinema/Courtesy: Everett Collection, p. 16; Unimedia International/Rex Features USA, p. 17; TM and Copyright © 20th Century Fox Flim Corp. All rights reserved/Courtesy: Everett Collection, p. 18; Orion/ The Kobal Collection/Francisco, Ricky, p. 19; Everett Collection, pp. 21, 25, 26, 41, 63, 79, 83; © Globe Photos, Inc., p. 23; © Kevin Winter/Getty Images, pp. 24, 38, 48, 59, 76, 84, 90, 94; © Kevin Mazur/WireImage/Getty Images, pp. 27, 51; Starstock/Photoshot/Everett Collection, p. 28; © Ron Galella/Wire Image/Getty Images, p. 29; 20th Century Fox/The Kobal Collection, p. 30; Mary Evans/Geffen Film Co/Ronald Grant/Everett Collection, p. 31; © MGM/Courtesy: Everett Collection, p. 33; Paramount/The Kobal Collection, p. 34; © Nancy R. Schiff/Hulton Archive/Getty Images, p. 36; © DMI/Time & Life Pictures/Getty Images, p. 37; Touchstone/ The Kobal Collection, p. 40; © James Aylott/Getty Images, p. 42; © Merrick Morton/New Line Cinema/Getty Images, p. 43; © Rob Brown/USA TODAY, p. 44; © Christophe d'Yvoire/Sygma/ CORBIS, p. 45; © Fotos International/Archive Photos/Getty Images, p. 47; © Patrick Hertzog/ AFP/Getty Images, p. 52; Artisan Pics/The Kobal Collection/Mountain, Peter, p. 53; © David Watts Jr./Dreamstime.com, p. 54; © Patrick Camboulive/Sygma/CORBIS, p. 55; Paramount Pictures/Mandalay Pictures/The Kobal Collection/Coote, Clive, p. 56; © Mirek Towski/DMI/ Time & Life Pictures/Getty Images, p. 57; © CD SE RF/ZBP/ZUMA Press, p. 58; © Miramax/ Courtesy: Everett Collection, p. 60; Alex J. Berliner/BEImages/Rex Features USA, p. 61; © Express Newspapers/Hulton Archive/Getty Images, p. 64; © Robert Hanashiro/USA TODAY, p. 66; Library of Congress (LC-B2-5000-14), p. 67; © Dan MacMedan/USA TODAY, p. 68; © Robert Deutsch/USA TODAY, p. 70; Walt Disney Pictures/The Kobal Collection, pp. 71, 92; AP Photo/Chris Pizzello, p. 72; © Franco Origlia/USA TODAY, p. 74; © Columbia/ Courtesy: Everett Collection, p. 77; © Warner Brothers/Courtesy: Everett Collection, pp. 78, 81; © Todd Plitt/USA TODAY, p. 80; © Walt Disney/Courtesy: Everett Collection, p. 82; © DreamWorks/Courtesy: Everett Collection, p. 87; Peter Mountain/© Universal/Courtesy: Everett Collection, p. 89; © Martin Bureau/AFP/Getty Images, p. 95; © GV Cruz/WireImage/ Getty Images, p. 96; © Peter Mountain/Columbia Pictures/ZUMA Press, p. 97.

Front cover: AP Photo/Joel Ryan.

Back cover: © Dan MacMedan/USA TODAY.

ABOUT THE AUTHOR

Matt Doeden is a writer and editor who lives in New Prague, Minnesota. After earning degrees in journalism and psychology from Minnesota State University-Mankato, he began his career as a sports writer. Since then, he's spent nearly a decade writing and editing high-interest nonfiction, with more than fifty titles to his name on topics that range from extreme sports to military equipment to graphic novels. In the Sports Heroes and Legends series, his titles include *Tiger Woods*, *Dale Earnhardt Jr.*, and *Lance Armstrong*. His Motor Mania titles include *Crazy Cars* and *Lowriders*. Among his other books are *Green Day* and *Will Smith*.